Anonymous

Celebration of the one hundredth Anniversary of the Birth-Day of William Ellery Channing

Anonymous

Celebration of the one hundredth Anniversary of the Birth-Day of William Ellery Channing

ISBN/EAN: 9783337146177

Printed in Europe, USA, Canada, Australia, Japan

Cover: Foto ©ninafisch / pixelio.de

More available books at **www.hansebooks.com**

CELEBRATION

OF THE

ONE HUNDREDTH ANNIVERSARY

OF THE

Birth-Day

OF

WILLIAM ELLERY CHANNING,

AT

THE CHURCH OF THE SAVIOUR,

AND AT

THE ACADEMY OF MUSIC,

Brooklyn, N. Y.,

Tuesday and Wednesday, April 6 and 7, 1880.

BOSTON:
GEO. H. ELLIS, 101 MILK STREET.
1880.

Printed and Stereotyped by Geo. H. Ellis, 101 Milk St., Boston.

CONTENTS.

	PAGE
INTRODUCTION,	5
OPENING SERVICES,	9
Order of Exercises,	9
Prayer of Rev. Rufus Ellis, D.D.,	9
Discourse of Rev. A. P. Peabody, D.D.,	10
MEMORIAL MEETING,	28
Prayer of Rev. F. W. Holland,	28
Remarks of Rev. A. P. Putnam, D.D., Chairman,	29
Remarks of Rev. F. A. Farley, D.D.,	32
Remarks of Rev. J. B. Thomas, D.D.,	42
Remarks of Rev. Dr. J. W. Buckley,	48
Centennial Ode, by Rev. J. W. Chadwick,	53
Remarks of Mr. Oliver Johnson,	58
Memorial Hymn, by Rev. William Newell, D.D.,	63
Remarks of Rev. C. H. Hall, D.D.,	65
Remarks of Rev. A. D. Mayo,	71
Remarks of Rev. H. R. Nye,	84
Remarks of Rabbi Gustav Gottheil,	86
Remarks of Rev. H. W. Foote,	90
SOCIAL FESTIVAL,	93
MEETING AT THE ACADEMY OF MUSIC,	94
Mr. A. A. Low, President,	97
Hymn, "O God, we praise Thee, and confess,"	98
Prayer by Rev. George C. Miln,	98
Address by Rev. Rufus Ellis, D.D.,	99
Address by Rev. Robert Collyer,	108
Address by Rev. J. M. Pullman, D.D.,	115
Hymn, "Come, Kingdom of our God,"	119
Address by Mr. George W. Curtis,	120

CONTENTS.

	PAGE
Address by Rev. C. N. Sims, D.D., . . .	130
Address by Rev. Henry Ward Beecher, . . .	133
Hymn, "O North, with all thy vales of green,"	149
Benediction, ...	150
APPENDIX, ...	151
Letter from Rev. George G. Channing,	151
Letter from Elizabeth P. Channing, . . .	152
Letter from Rev. William H. Channing, . .	152
Letter from Rev. Charles T. Brooks, .	152
Letter from Mary E. Dewey, ...	153
Letter from Rev. Samuel Osgood, D.D., LL.D.,	153
Letter from Mr. George Ripley, . . .	154
Letter from Rev. H. W. Bellows, D.D., . . .	156
Letter from Rev. James Martineau, D.D., LL.D., .	157
Letter from Rev. Phillips Brooks, D.D., . . .	159
Letter from Rev. William Newell, D.D., .	160
Letter from Rev. John Cordner, LL.D., .	161
Letter from Rev. F. H. Hedge, D.D, . . .	162
Letter from Rev. Ephraim Turland, England, .	164
Letter from Rev. C. A. Bartol, D.D., . . .	165
Letter from Rev. Robert Spear, England,	166
Letter from Rev. Thomas Hill, D.D., LL.D., .	167
Letter from Bishop Joseph Ferencz, Transylvania,	168
Letter from Professor David Swing, . .	169
Letter from Rev. E. M. Stone, ...	170
Letter from Rev. Andrew Chalmers, England, .	171
Letter from Rev. George H. Emerson, D.D.,	171
Letter from Rev. William G. Eliot, D.D., . .	172
Letter from Dr. Franz von Holtzendorff, Bavaria,	173
Letter from Rev. C. C. Everett, D.D., . . .	173
Letter from the Dutch Protestant Association, Holland,	174
Letter from Rev. C. C. Sewall, ...	175
Letter from Hon. Samuel E. Sewall, . .	176
Letter from Rev. George W. Hosmer, D.D.,	178
Letter from Rev. John Cotton Smith, D.D.,	178
Letter from Rev. John H. Morison, D.D.,	179
Letter from Friends in Hungary, . .	180
Letter from Mr. John Fretwell, England, .	182
Resolutions of Churches in Brooklyn, .	199
Extracts from the Press, ...	201

INTRODUCTION.

The following pages present a detailed record of the Memorial Services, held at Brooklyn, N.Y., in honor of the One Hundredth Anniversary of the birthday of William Ellery Channing. The plan of such a celebration was brought to the attention of the Trustees of the Church of the Saviour, in that city, as early in the year as Sunday, January 11. The matter was more fully considered at a meeting of the Board, held at the house of the President, Isaac H. Frothingham, Esq., on the evening of February 3, after it had been found that a sufficient number of able speakers would be ready to participate in the proceedings of the occasion to insure success.

The enterprise was regarded with earnest favor, and a Committee of Arrangements was appointed to take it in hand, and carry it forward to completion. This Committee was subsequently enlarged by additions from the other Unitarian churches in the city, as appears in the list appended to the circular of invitation. The action of the Trustees was heartily approved by the congregation of the Church of the Saviour, at a meeting which took place immediately after the morning service, Sunday, February 8. In the forenoon of the following day, the ladies of the Society assembled, and entered into arrangements for the social festival, and for the decoration of the Church and Chapel. The plans of the Committee having been largely matured, the following circular was sent to Unitarian societies far and near; and another, slightly changed in form, was mailed to a large number of persons of all sects and communions in and out of the city:—

BROOKLYN, N.Y., March 12, 1880.

DEAR SIR:

Wednesday, the 7th of April next, being the one hundredth anniversary of the birthday of

WILLIAM ELLERY CHANNING,

it is proposed here, in this city, as in many other places, to mark the occasion with suitable public services in honor of the memory of that illustrious man.

INTRODUCTION.

An opening service will be held in the Church of the Saviour, corner of Pierrepont Street and Monroe Place, Brooklyn Heights, Tuesday evening, April 6, at 7.45 o'clock, Rev. A. P. Peabody, D.D., of Cambridge, Mass., preaching the sermon.

The next day there will be, in the same place, at 10 A.M., a commemorative meeting, to be addressed by ministers and laymen of the immediate vicinity, and of other cities and States, who are of widely different theological views and ecclesiastical relations, but who yet all deeply venerate the name of Channing. Some of the surviving personal friends or acquaintances of the revered preacher and philanthropist will be present and will speak, and letters will be read from others who may not be able to attend.

At 2 o'clock P.M., a lunch will be served to the guests at a social festival to be held under the direction of the ladies of the Society, in the Chapel and Basement Hall of the Church.

In the evening of the same day, Wednesday, the 7th, at 7.45 o'clock, there will be a public meeting at the Academy of Music, Montague Street, at which Mr. A. A. Low will preside, and addresses will be made by Rev. Rufus Ellis, D.D., pastor of the First Church, Boston; Mr. George W. Curtis, Rev. E. H. Chapin, D.D., Rev. Robert Collyer, and others. There will be choir and congregational singing.

Among those who have already expressed their intention to join in this celebration may be named, in addition to those who are mentioned above, Rev. Drs. F. A. Farley, Rufus P. Stebbins, and Samuel Osgood; Rev. Messrs. F. W. Holland, R. R. Shippen, A. D. Mayo, H. R. Nye, S. R. Calthrop, Henry W. Foote, Joseph May, J. W. Chadwick, S. H. Camp, J. L. Seward, and other well-known clergymen.

You and your friends are cordially invited to be present at these meetings. Pastors and delegates coming from the out-of-town churches to which this circular is sent, and wishing or purposing to remain in the city during the celebration, will confer a favor by reporting themselves at the Tuesday evening or Wednesday morning meeting, to any of the members of the subjoined committees from various societies in Brooklyn, that the hospitalities of the occasion may be duly extended to them. We also request any such parties, so far as it may be convenient to them, to forward to us beforehand the names of those of their number who are likely to be with us.

Sincerely yours,
ALFRED P. PUTNAM,
Pastor of the Church of the Saviour.

Reception Committee. — Isaac H. Frothingham, Joseph R. Blossom, and James Littlejohn, of the Board of Trustees of the Church, with others, ladies and gentlemen, whose names will be announced hereafter.

Committee of Arrangements. — A. P. Putnam, *Chairman;* Alfred T. White, Isaac H. Cary, Jr., Sylvester Swain, Josiah B. Blossom, E. A. Doty, W. H. Cromwell, E. M. Whiting, J. H. Hebert, John W. Wood, Ethelbert M. Low, D. B. Halstead, William Potts, W. C. Gardner, Alfred P. Dix, Hersey Brown,

T. F. Taylor, Robert Foster, Joseph Lyman, B. T. Frothingham, E. M. Wheeler, W. A. Butler, Richard Arnold, T. C. Wallace, Gustavus Coombs.

Several sub-committees were formed out of the general Committee of Arrangements, Messrs. Nelson G. Carman, Jr., Chauncey E. Low, and others acting with them, to have special charge of the matters of Music, Finance, Printing, Advertising, and various things pertaining to the meeting at the Academy.

The idea or purpose which had early manifested itself, of making the celebration large and inclusive in its spirit and scope, was soon still more fully revealed; and people and churches of the neighborhood and the public at large, without regard to creed or name, were cordially asked to join in the celebration. Ministers and laymen, of evangelical and liberal denominations indiscriminately, were invited to speak at the meetings. The response from all sides was most gratifying. It was found that, however widely men were separated from Dr. Channing in the direction of conservatism or radicalism, yet all recognized some vital point of agreement or sympathy with him. To bring out this latent and universal feeling and let it find full expression was the strong desire of the Committee.

They were glad to find that their policy was universally approved. The meetings, however varied their utterances, were wonderfully harmonious in spirit. Each speaker expressed freely and fearlessly his honest thought, yet there was nothing said to give pain or disturb the good feeling of the occasion from beginning to end. Every voice waked responsive echoes, and the interest and enthusiasm of the crowds that were in attendance increased till the close of the last meeting. The memorial meeting of Wednesday morning not only witnessed the presence of many who had personally known Dr. Channing or heard him preach, some of them having listened to the first sermons which he preached in New York; but it was also particularly rich in letters and speeches of reminiscences of the great and good man whom all had met to honor.

A pathetic interest attaches to the letter from Dr. Osgood, which may be found in the Appendix. The Chairman knowing his earnest desire and purpose to join in the celebration, called for him at the morning meeting, but in vain. After the occasion had passed, the now published letter was received, from which it appeared that his absence was due to the fatigue consequent upon the delivery of an address before the New York Historical Society on the previous evening, his subject being the Life, Character, and Work of Channing. It is a touching circumstance that such was the theme of his last public utterance; for a few days later the community was startled and saddened by the announcement of the death of this able preacher and eminent Christian scholar, this broad-minded, gentle-hearted, pure, and faithful man of God. The larger audience in the Academy was likewise disappointed in the absence of Rev. E. H. Chapin, D.D., who was also debarred from attendance by serious illness, but sent before the celebration his sincere regrets and earnest good wishes.

The pulpit of the Church of the Saviour was occupied on Sunday, April 4, by Rev. A. D. Mayo, of Springfield, Mass., whose sermons, morning and evening, the one on "New Saints for the New Republic," and the other on "Our Common Christianity," closed with tributes to Dr. Channing, and formed a fitting introduction to the memorial services of the week.

Thanks are due and are given to all who aided the enterprise by their sympathy or active co-operation: to the friends whose addresses and letters constituted the great interest of the occasion; to Mr. John Fretwell, the well-known English Unitarian, through whose kindness most welcome communications came to us from distant countries; to the Rev. Dr. H. W. Bellows, and also the Church of the Messiah, of New York, for special favors and remembrances referred to elsewhere in these pages; to the local papers for their words of generous encouragement; and to Mr. George Hannah, Librarian of the Long Island Historical Society, Mr. Oliver Johnson, Rev. H. W. Foote, and others, for their valuable assistance in connection with this published Report. The report of the speeches and prayers of the various meetings was made by the accomplished stenographer, Mr. T. J. Ellinwood; and each address is printed in this pamphlet as revised by the speaker. In two or three cases, by request, some point of peculiar interest is more fully presented in the written than it was in the oral account.

OPENING SERVICES.

The church, at the appointed hour of service, was filled with people of all denominations in the city, a large number of representative clergymen and laymen of the different sects and neighboring churches being in the audience.

ORDER OF EXERCISES.

1. Voluntary on the Organ.
2. Anthem.
3. Prayer, by Rev. Rufus Ellis, D.D.
4. Te Deum.
5. Reading of the Scriptures, by Rev. Joseph May. (Rom. viii., 1–10; I. Cor. xii., 4–27; xiii., 1–13.)
6. Hymn, "Oh, sometimes gleams upon our sight."
7. Sermon, by Rev. A. P. Peabody, D.D.
8. Silent Prayer, followed by the Lord's Prayer, chanted by the Choir.
9. Hymn, "O God, the darkness roll away."
10. Benediction, by Rev. Dr. Peabody.

The pastor, in giving out the last hymn, announced the meetings of the following day. The prayer and sermon of the evening are herewith published: —

PRAYER BY REV. RUFUS ELLIS, D.D.

Not without thee, O our Father, are we met together. May thy Spirit move upon our hearts; for, except thy Spirit move upon our hearts, they are but as barren clay, and can bring forth no good fruit. Thou art near to us, — nearer to us than any of thy children. May we be near to thee in our hours of sorrow and of joy, and of glad remembrance. May thy heavens be opened above us, and may we know that we are compassed about by a great cloud of witnesses. May we give thee humble and hearty thanks for those who being dead yet live and speak to us, and that their voices are still heard in the world and felt in our hearts.

Oh, grant unto us to love thee as much as thy children have loved thee in times past. Grant unto us also the fulness and the blessedness and the power of thy present Spirit, that signs and wonders may still be wrought in our world; that, as we look up, and gratefully and fondly recall those that have served thee in their day and generation, and chiefly one whose memory is dear to our hearts in this hour, we too may learn to call thee our Father, and to follow after thee as dear and faithful children.

May the word which shall be spoken to us in this hour be thine own word,— that word which doth not return unto thee void,— that we may go forth and serve thee more faithfully, and be indeed a true household before thee, seeking always those things which are above, and those things which are helpful unto thy children.

And unto thee, the Ever-blessed and Holy One, shall be everlasting praise, in him who loved us and who died for us. *Amen.*

COMMEMORATIVE DISCOURSE

By REV. A. P. PEABODY, D.D.

Psalm cxii., 6.—" The righteous shall be in everlasting remembrance."

No religious communion in this country can ever have presented a more goodly array of illustrious names than American Unitarianism when it commenced its separate career. Among Channing's seniors were Freeman, Ware, Bancroft, Kirkland, Thayer, the Abbots,— the best known among a cluster of faithful, holy men, whose memory still lingers — sacred and precious — with a generation that has sprung up since they passed away. Of those who were within a few years his coevals, it is enough to specify Tuckerman, who became great by being " the least of all and the servant of all"; Buckminster, the golden-mouthed; the saintly Lowell; Nichols, unequalled — in the recollection of those who knew him — in glowing thought and eloquent discourse on themes of largest, loftiest import; Parker, the model pastor; Norton, whose demonstration of the genuineness of the Gospels has maintained an impregnable front against the scepticism of half a century. A few years later came the younger Abbot, the younger Wares, Greenwood, Walker, Palfrey, Sparks, Gannett,— all names of reverence. Among these, Channing undoubtedly had his peers in learning, eloquence, the cure of souls, or adaptation to some specific Christian work, and certainly in sanctity of spirit, pureness of life, and consecration to the service of God and man. He is pre-eminent among them — first among equals — by the breadth of the field over which his labor extended, by the wide range of his influence, by the copiousness of his writings, and, especially, by his foremost place in the exposition and defence of the faith which he held in common with them. Among them all he still retains the primacy. No religious writer of our age has at this day a stronger hold than he on cultivated and serious minds, not only in our own country, but in England and on the continent of Europe. His influence has gained rather than lost with the lapse of time. It is felt even more in other denominations than in his own. He has borne an essential part in shaping the theology of large sections of the Church universal; and among those who sympathize most fervently with the spirit of this anniversary are not a few members of communions which in his lifetime would have hesitated to include him within the Christian pale. To him do we owe it that, were he with us now, he would find little to dissent from in the theology of the divines who have succeeded his most vehement antagonists.

In our estimate of his service to his race, we may take no small account of the blended sweetness and power of his personal presence and intercourse. In my early life, as a teacher for a few months of one of his children, I was often at his house and his table, and once — his guest for a night — I had the unspeakable privilege of uniting with him in the morning service of prayer for and with his family. In all that I remember of him, it was as if "an angel spake." That thin, worn countenance, luminous with thought and quivering with emotion; those solemn, benignant eyes, which seemed as if they were always turned heavenward, yet as if they looked right into the soul of him with whom he was conversing; that slender thread of a voice, trembling like the chords of an Æolian harp with every breath of the spirit, with modulations so delicate that you might have almost interpreted his words had they been uttered in an unknown tongue, — I can see and hear him now, though with the interval of well-nigh half a century. He spoke only on great themes; his soul was filled with them, enwrapped in them; and none who listened could go from him unmoved. Nor were the listeners few. As a chronic invalid, for many years he seldom appeared in public; but in the quiet of his study there was daily conference as to the interests and needs of the Church, the country, the world, — not only on the deep things of God, but equally on the questions of the day, national politics, slavery, pauperism, plans of usefulness, drifts of public opinion and feeling, impending dangers, movements of rival parties as to the administration of the State. But with him the distinction between things secular and sacred was obliterated. The balance of the sanctuary was never out of his hand. The affairs of this life were to him eternal interests. His only state-policy was loyalty to God. His only measure of public conduct was the rule of eternal right. No minister, no Christian, could fail to be enlightened, strengthened, gladdened by intercourse with him; and who can say how many men in public and busy life derived from him their profoundest sense of responsibility and duty, and were by him inspired with noble purpose, and energized for unselfish, faithful service of their country and their race?

The political influence of his writings cannot be overestimated. He had the prophet's foreseeing vision, and often wrote in advance what afterward became history,— history, too, that has been developing itself down to the present day. His letter on the question of the Annexation of Texas needs only the change of tense to be inscribed among the country's annals. An early residence in the South gave him an advanced place among the anti-slavery men of the North, and his voice was last heard in public in that sacred cause. Among those who on all other subjects sympathized with him, he long stood almost alone; but in the lapse of years he won many strong minds and warm hearts to plead with him for the victims of tyranny and oppression; and, as the final conflict drew near, not a few of the leaders in opinion and action found support and encouragement in his brave words, which, when they fell from his pen, were as "the voice of one crying in the wilderness."

The same standard of eternal right, the same solemn sense of divine things, which shaped his political opinions and influence, gave character to what in other hands might have been mere literature, but in his could be only a wider scale of notes on the one unvarying key. Thus his essays on Milton and on Napoleon are as intensely religious as his sermons, and scarce less directly so. His sole purpose in them was, on the one hand, to place in their true light the traits that constitute the glory of humanity as emancipated, empowered, and ennobled by Christ, and, on the other hand, to exhibit the intrinsic littleness and baseness of what is vulgarly accounted great, if it be great for self, and not for man,— to destroy, and not to save and bless.

As a preacher, Dr. Channing first attracted notice by his subdued and chastened seriousness. His early sermons were emotional rather than thoughtful, meditative rather than hortatory, as of one who stood on the mount and within the veil, and whose cry was, "Come up hither." This characteristic belonged equally to his entire life as a preacher. But more and more, with added years, profound and vigorous thought blended with the ever-present spirit of devotion. He became master of forceful reasoning, trenchant rejoinder, and luculent demonstration; and our language has no more perfect specimens of argumentative sermons — every assailable point guarded, every avenue of attack fully manned — than his sermons on the evidences of Christianity, and on the doctrines which he regarded as its central and vital truths. But his logic was always aglow in the vestal flame of piety and love. He contended, never for his own dogma maintained in the pride of opinion or in the vain glory of logomachy, but always for what he deemed the truth of God, — for what to his own heart had been unspeakably precious, and which it was therefore his fervent desire to render sanctifying truth to the immortal souls under the wordfall of his lips. To sympathetic hearers there was no need of the "Let us pray" at the close of a sermon. It had been anticipated when he began, and had not for one moment lost its stress. Thus, while his eloquence won the suffrages of those who listened only to admire and praise, it was his devout hearers who best appreciated the union of beauty, grace, and fervor in his pulpit utterance.

His manner in the pulpit bore a close resemblance to that of his conversation. His gestures were few, simple, spontaneous. His voice was thin and seemed feeble, yet it was clear, sonorous, and penetrating; and, while those near him no more than heard him well, his enunciation was so distinct, and his emphasis so just and strong, that in the breathless stillness which he always commanded his remotest hearers can seldom have lost a word. It was the charm of his oratory that it was in no sense oratory. There was none of the self-consciousness almost inevitable in a public speaker, but the simple consciousness, "I have a message from God, and how am I straitened until it be delivered!"

His written style owes its attraction and its hold upon the reader to that same absence of self-consciousness. He never aimed to write well, and therefore, being the man he was, he could not but write pre-eminently well. The grace and beauty in his soul needed no elaboration to clothe them in faultless and rhythmical form. His conversance with the best English authors and his thorough classical culture ensured for him free command of fitting words; his delicate taste had its counterpart in a diction always pure and elegant; and the directness and simplicity of his aim saved him from obscureness, and enabled him to be always perspicuous, even when most profound. With much of the mystic element in his devotion, and, no doubt, often burdened with feelings that were not thoughts, with groanings of the spirit too deep to be uttered, he seems never to have forgotten that there are two parties to written discourse, and that the writer — if he would teach, inspire, and help his fellow-men — is bound never to transcend the receptivity of his readers.

As regards Dr. Channing's theological position and influence, it must be borne in mind that he is responsible only for what he thought, said, wrote, and was, and in no sense or degree for opinions which he would have repudiated, even with horror, or for tendencies on which he turned his back, and not his face. No man is to be held to account for more of the future than that to which he helped to give shape; no leader, for directions in which he did not lead. The Unitarian denomination, in common with others, yet I think not more than others, has been largely and injuriously affected from two widely different sources of influence, one of which was opened toward the close of Channing's life, the other not till very recently. I say that the Unitarian has not been thus affected more than other denominations; yet my words will hardly seem to justify themselves at first thought, and for a very obvious reason. In most religious bodies there has been an inflexible standard of orthodoxy, and the clergy who have swerved from it have been driven from their own communion, and have — though really not of us — sought refuge in ours, which, because of its lack of a required profession of faith, has borne to the rest of the Christian world very much the same relation in which Texas, before her admission to the Union, stood to the States whose nondescript exiles chose it for their home. The only churches in Christendom — except ours — which keep dissenters from their creed within their pale are the Lutheran Church in Continental Europe, now for the most part merged in the German National Church, and the Established Church of England; and in both of these the tendencies adverse to the Christianity of the New Testament have had full and broad development, creating in the latter a Texas of no mean extent, and in the former one far exceeding in dimensions the realm that has colonized it.

Of the sources to which I refer, the first is the study of German philosophy and theology. When Dr. Channing retired from the active ministry, there were but two or three Unitarian clergymen, and they persistently strong conservatives, who were known to be conversant with the German language, which had not then a place even in the curriculum of Harvard University. About that time, the advent of Dr. Follen, his ability as a teacher of his native tongue, and the fascination inseparable from a man whom none could know without admiring and loving him, gave a strong impulse to the study of German, especially among the younger members of the clerical profession. They found thus opened to them a bewildering range of thought and criticism, entirely novel, and so utterly un-English that it had hardly begun to be translated or transfused in England. The very cloudiness of much of this literature and philosophy gave it only the greater prestige ; for a misty atmosphere enhances the apparent height and magnitude of what it enwraps, and conceals its lack of foundation. The consequence of this new departure was a (so-called) transcendental philosophy (which had no exclusive title to that name, unless it were because it transcended the understanding of all but its adepts), with a rationalistic interpretation of Scripture, and, notably, of the narrative portions of the New Testament. In this movement, Dr. Channing neither led nor followed. So far as he had any German affinities, it was with the pietists of an earlier age ; and nothing was more abhorrent from his whole spirit and character than a philosophy which should either repudiate or supersede faith. Yet he could not but have had strong sympathy with the spiritual beauty and loveliness of some of his circle, for whom the faith of their childhood had wrought its sanctifying work before it became obscured or impaired.

Transcendentalism, after a brief ascendency, forsook a climate never congenial to it, yet not without leaving a trail of scepticism ; and this spirit of thinnest air has been succeeded by the earth-demon of self-styled physical science, which yet is not science, but in part natural history, in part hypothesis. For what it is, I hold it in reverent regard. It is no less man's duty than his privilege so to subdue the earth as to make it tributary to mental and spiritual no less than to physical uses,—to do all that in him lies to enlarge his knowledge of the outward world, till he is fully prepared to shape his knowedge into science. But the physicist or the naturalist is not therefore a philosopher or a theologian. Because he knows all about bugs or trees, he is not therefore competent to be oracular about the soul and God. Because he can trace orderly processes in nature, he is not authorized to dethrone the Creator, whether by denying his existence, or by representing him as the helpless slave of an automatic universe. Equally little right has he to propound materialistic theories of mind, thought, soul, while he admits that he has not made in this region a single discovery, but merely avers the non-existence and the impossibility of a realm of being outside the range of the microscope and beyond the reach of the scalpel. This agnosticism, though not avowed in the pulpit in express terms, is not without its influence in lowering the tone of religious belief and devotional feeling, in casting doubts on the providence of God and on the reality of prayer, in discrediting the distinctively Divine element in Christianity, and in subjecting all spiritual phenomena to the laws of a necessary and spontaneous development.

These two tendencies, from sources extraneous to our denomination and our country, cannot without the grossest injustice be ascribed to the fathers of American Unitarianism, or to anything in the religious system of which they were the expositors and defenders. They belong to their respective times. One of these sources has ceased to flow; the other is already ebbing.

Dr. Channing's influence was most emphatic and intense in behalf of the right of free inquiry,—a right universally admitted now, but in his early days almost as universally called in question. Dissent from established creeds was regarded as hardly less than a crime, not, indeed, punishable by the law, but visited with denial of the Christian name, with exclusion from Christian ordinances, and often with social ostracism. Dr. Channing vindicated private judgment and individual opinion as the right, and, even more, the duty of every Christian. He would, no doubt, had there been occasion, have vindicated the right of sincere denial, and have claimed tolerance and amnesty for honest unbelief.

But his concern was with liberty within the fold of Christ, not beyond it,— with the use which the Christian should make of the oracles of God,— of the revelation in and through Jesus of Nazareth. No man would have been more ready than he to say to the assailant of the authority of the Divine Teacher,— to the unbeliever in the veracity of the Christian record,— "You have the same right to your position that I have to mine; but your right is to occupy your own position, not mine. Your place as an honest man is outside of the Church, not in it; your part, open attack, not covert treachery."

Dr. Channing was, first and chief of all, a Christian,— a Christian in belief, dissenting from received creeds solely because he interpreted the words of Christ, and of those who best knew the mind of Christ, in a sense adverse to their teaching,— a Christian, too, in the inmost depths of his heart, honoring Jesus as the Incarnate Word of God, uttering his name only with tender reverence, deeming it his highest blessedness to obey and follow him on earth, and to be united with him in heaven. He received Christ's own testimony concerning himself, "My Father is greater than I"; but in his faith Jesus held a place second only to God. For the greater part of his life he maintained the doctrine commonly, though not with entire accuracy, called Arian, according to which Jesus had his separate being before all worlds. I find no proof in his writings that he ever renounced this belief; though, in his later years, there is reason to think, not that he lapsed into humanitarianism, but that he rose to the conception of Christ as even more intimately one with God, as representing all of the Divine that can be made human, so that he would have found no reason to object on doctrinal grounds to that spurious reading, yet truly apostolic and Christian idea, "God manifest in the flesh,"— a faith which it would be hard to discriminate from that of many professed

Trinitarians of our day, some of whom lament that the term *Trinity* ever found currency in the Church.

This positive Christian faith rested with him, as could not but have been the case, primarily on his own intuition and experience. To one who had felt its worth and power as he had, the Gospel was its own sufficient evidence. But he none the less attached essential importance to the attestation of prophecy and miracle. It would have seemed to him the greatest of all miracles that the advent of our Lord should have been unannounced, unheralded, unattended by manifest tokens of the unshared pre-eminence which he held among the sons of men. He, therefore, held the form of Christianity portrayed in the Gospels as sacred and Divine. He believed in the historical Christ as standing in immediate relation with his Church; and how far his faith in the personal Saviour was from becoming less clear and emphatic toward the close of his life, we may best learn from a sentence in his very last public address, written but a few weeks before his death: "The doctrine of the 'Word made flesh' shows us God uniting Himself most intimately with our nature, manifesting Himself in a human form for the very end of making us partakers of his own perfection."

In reviewing Channing's life, we are bound to rake among the ashes, though we would not for the world rekindle the fires, of the Trinitarian controversy. Peaceful as are the thoughts which now cluster around his memory, the time was, within the recollection of the elder among us, when the only associations that his name suggested were those of an ardent, adroit, and subtile controversialist; and for years those who did not know him personally knew little else about him.

The beginnings of his ministry showed neither disposition nor aptitude for controversy; but he was forced into a polemic attitude,—at least he was compelled to stand on the defensive, and in such warfare defence means attack, and can mean nothing else.

The churches of New England had, from the time of the Revolutionary War, been in a quiescent state, with little religious life, though outwardly prosperous. A mild and not very well-defined Calvinism was the prevailing creed; but it was maintained so loosely that Arminian and Unitarian opinions, held to a considerable extent among both the clergy and the laity, excited no general alarm or oppugnancy. About the close of the first decade of this century, there was an intensely strong movement toward a more stringent orthodoxy, and at the same time toward a higher tone of religious life and a more earnest and efficient propagandism. The establishment of Park Street Church, and the occupancy of its pulpit by a divine of unsurpassed ability, zeal, and energy, made Boston the centre of this movement. The type of orthodoxy represented there was not by any means genial. Intense stress was laid on the utter depravity of man, as the consequence of Adam's guilt; on the atonement, as the infliction upon Christ of agony equivalent to the punishment due to the sins of the entire host of the redeemed; and on the election of a certain portion of the human race to salvation from eternal torment, and that, not because of their faith or good works, which were the consequence, not the cause, of the Divine decree in their favor. It must be acknowledged that in this theology the paternal character of God was hardly recognized, nay, was even virtually denied, and ransomed men were rather bought off from the wrath of God than saved by his love.

Channing's profound piety was of an entirely different type. With him, the divine fatherhood was the fundamental doctrine of the Gospel. He believed in an atonement; but it was the reconciling of man to God, not of God to man. "God was in Christ, reconciling the world unto himself."

Human nature he regarded as absolutely pure and stainless, till corrupted by the individual man's departure from his primitive innocence. He ignored not only the taint of Adam's guilt, but equally the sad heritage of evil propensities from nearer progenitors, which, a few years later, a sounder philosophy would undoubtedly have constrained him to acknowledge. These doctrines were to him not mere articles of an objective creed; they were subjective,— portions of his religious consciousness, the very central truths of his personal faith, incorporated with all his devotional feeling. In advocating them, he was but pleading the cause of his own soul. His oppugnancy to the doctrines maintained by the (so-called) Orthodox party was vehement, burning, indignant, and found utterance in the most vivid rhetoric, often severe and scathing, though never assuming the form of personal invective, and in the intensity of indignation never lapsing into anger. His earnestness and fervor ensured for him, without his seeking it, the leader's place. His church was thronged. His services as a preacher were sought on all occasions when a blow was to be struck for the liberal faith, when a new ministry was to be inaugurated in a distant city, or when an antagonist worthy of his steel was to be encountered. His directly controversial discourses and essays were few; but in them his words were battles,—often too highly pitched for our quiet times, but not so in what, as we look back on those days, seems the war of giants. Those were conflicts in which no quarter was asked or given. There is no need of disguising the fact,— the questions at issue were not of more or less, but between radically opposite theologies. Nor can there be any doubt that, while neither party confessed defeat, each did essential service to the other, in modifying extreme views, and in creating the middle ground on which the more liberal among the Orthodox and the more conservative Unitarians find themselves with many points of sympathy and union, and, wherein they differ, with no harshness of mutual repugnancy. There are, it must be admitted, passages in some of Channing's sermons which we would gladly see stricken out, were they not of value as historical waymarks; but there was abundant reason for them when they were uttered: they were adapted to meet postulates and arguments which seemed to provoke only the strongest antagonism; and it would be hard to say which side had the advantage in coolness, moderation, and forbearance.

The doctrines thus contended for in the heat of controversy underlie all Dr. Channing's writings. With no little iteration, yet with an ever fresh power of argument and appeal, the fatherhood of God and the dignity of human nature are his unvarying themes. No matter what the nominal subject, they occupy the foreground. They strike the key-note to his great sermon on War, which led to the formation of the first Peace Society in the world. They inspired his earnest co-operation with Dr. Tuckerman in his ministry to the poor. They are the mainspring of his antagonism to slavery, which he abhorred, not for the physical evils which it involved, but because it imbruted God's image in the enslaved, and defaced it in those who assumed the ownership of fellow-beings standing on the same plane with themselves in the love and mercy of the common Father.

These great doctrines are no longer claimed as the heritage of any one sect, but are now more and more the transcendent truths recognized as primal under every form of Christian doctrine. The untempered wrath of God is no longer preached anywhere. The atonement is regarded by all alike as the work of Divine love. Christians of every name lay equal stress on our Saviour's declaration, "God so loved the world that he sent his only begotten Son." We claim not, by any means, for Channing an unshared agency in this revolution of opinion and feeling. But when we consider how largely he is read, and by persons of every shade of Christian belief, we cannot but think that to him is due no small portion of the intenerating influence, which has been felt in the whole American Church, in mollifying harsh creeds, in toning down dissension among Christians, and in restoring the love of God and the love of man to their primacy as the rule equally of faith and of practice,— as determining no less what shall be believed than what shall be felt and done by those who would be the followers of Jesus.

This centennial anniversary marks a signal change in our theological world. I was in New York, and took part in the services held there in honor of Channing a few days after his death. The occasion was exclusively denominational. We of his faith were deeply moved, and felt that the greatest among us had fallen; but there was no outside sympathy. We did not expect that any but ourselves should own the bereavement, or bring a monumental offering. Now there are those of all the churches who unite to do him honor. He is regarded no longer as the standard-bearer of a sect, but as a high-priest of God, a close follower of Christ, a champion of the oppressed and enslaved, a friend of the poor, a lover of his race. These are the titles on which we claim for him an honored memory; this, the only record that he would have craved. But whence this change? To what is it to be ascribed? Not to the growth of Unitarianism, not to the diminished zeal, the enfeebled piety, or the waning loyalty of other bodies of Christians, but to an enhanced appreciation of character as compared with creed,— to the growing conviction that all honest and brave Christian work, wrought in the love of God and man, has its blessed record in heaven, and should be held in dear regard and sacred reverence by the whole Church on earth.

As I look through what remains to us of Channing's life

and writings for some one pervading thought, sentiment, aim, purpose, which gives unity to his character, force to his influence, worth to his example, and by which "he being dead yet speaketh," it is loyalty to Christ. This is the inspiring theme of his earliest published sermon, preached at the ordination of his classmate, Rev. Dr. Codman, in which, after describing the Christian pastorate as it ought to be,— a pleading with men in the Saviour's stead to be reconciled to God,— he designates as its reward beyond all price, "With what joy will such a minister stand before the judgment-seat of Christ!" Almost his last utterance in public was the invocation, "Come, Friend, and Saviour of the race, who didst shed thy blood on the cross to reconcile man to man and earth to heaven!" It was the words of Christ that he asked to have read to him as he was passing through the shadow of death, and while they yet lingered on his ear he fell asleep.

Firm faith in Christ, and a tender, reverent love for him, equally characterized the leading divines who were Channing's intimate associates. The one precious name was ever on their lips. I am sure that there can never have been heard on this side heaven more glowing utterances than their wonted ascriptions of praise and gratitude to the Author of our salvation; and in separating from their fellow-Christians they felt that they were only drawing nearer to the heart of Christ.

The last half-century has given us no reason for a feebler faith or a less fervent love. As regards argument and evidence, Christianity has only gained, were it possible, a stronger position, and could ask no better championship than in the concessions, recantations, mutual refutations, and self-contradictions of its opponents. Its wealth of precept, doctrine, example, and promise, and its versatility of adaptation to the needs of mankind, seem inexhaustible, no less in the twilight, which we call the broad day of the ninteenth century, than in what we deem the twilight of the first. Christ's is still, in all that can constitute pre-eminence, the "name above every name." Nor is there any new phase of unbelief or scepticism, which makes a nearer approach to Christianity than did the (so-called) infidelity of earlier times. Its several existing types — even those that pretend to be new — are old. They have their antetypes, respectively, in the English Deists, in the French Encyclopædists, and in the materialism of Lucretius and the Epicurean school, this last at once the newest and the oldest. It is a false liberality which would claim for them or accede to them, under any conditions or circumstances, the Christian name. Those to whom the Christ of the Gospels is a congeries of myths, or a development of humanity which our age is outgrowing, or but one of a galaxy of wise and holy men, cannot honestly call themselves Christians, and we do them no kindness by abetting them in their falsity. Were it not that "the foundation of God standeth firm," they would bear the same relation to its corner-stone which Samson bore to the pillars of the house of Dagon. We are no more bound to affiliate ourselves with them than with the followers of Mohammed, or of Confucius, or of Buddha, who stand in fully as close an affinity as they to the Christian commonwealth. Mohammed had very nearly the same opinion of Christ which they are wont to avow; and they are very fond of naming Confucius and Buddha as at least Christ's equals, if not his superiors. This estimate it is their right to make, if they can make it honestly; and we are under sacred obligations, not only to accord to them what, indeed, is not ours to deny or withhold, entire liberty of opinion and utterance, but to honor them for their genius and learning, to esteem and love them for whatever of moral excellence there is in them, and to thank God that his good gifts are not and never have been confined exclusively to his Church. Indeed, we have the rule and spirit of our relation to truly wise and good men who are not Christians in our Saviour's own words: "Other sheep I have who are not of this fold. Them also I must bring, and they shall hear my voice, and there shall be one fold and one shepherd." He will bring them in his own good time, if not on earth, in heaven; but that is altogether a different matter from his flock's breaking down the fences of his fold, so that he shall have no need to bring in those who are outside of it. For the integrity of our portion of the Christian Church, whose very existence as a member of Christ's body is brought into imminent peril by the incursion of those who claim the name of Christian, yet deny and spurn the obvious, necessary, and essential contents of that name; and still more, for the sake of immortal souls that need for their life-way not a shifting, flickering light, but guiding rays as from a meridian sun,—"let us hold fast the profession of our faith without wavering." So shall be fulfilled in us those words of God through the Hebrew prophet: "Let them return unto thee; but return not thou unto them. And I will make thee unto this people a fenced brazen wall; and they shall fight against thee, but they shall not prevail against thee."

Let us commemorate the illustrious dead by taking up their line of march under the great Captain of our salvation; and, while with pious care we build their sepulchres, let their more precious and enduring memorial be our allegiance to the faith in which they lived and died, our consecration to the Saviour in whom, though dead, they live.

MEMORIAL MEETING.

The Memorial Meeting was held in the Church of the Saviour on the next day, Wednesday, April 7, at 10 A.M. The church was again crowded with representatives of all denominations. There were many present from the neighboring towns and cities. On and around the pulpit and tablets were rich and abundant floral decorations. The baptismal font was surmounted with a large and beautiful cross and star of flowers, a gift from the Church of the Messiah, New York. Directly in front of the pulpit, resting upon an easel, and facing the audience, was the fine portrait of Dr. Channing, by Ingham, kindly lent for the occasion by Dr. Bellows, its owner. The services were opened with a chant by the choir. Rev. Dr. A. P. Putnam, Chairman, then called upon Rev. F. W. Holland, former pastor of the church, to offer prayer.

PRAYER BY REV. F. W. HOLLAND.

O thou who art nearer to us than we dare to dream, more willing to bless than we are to seek thy blessing, visiting us continually by thy providence, thy Son, thy Spirit, we thank thee that, having sent to thy church apostles and prophets, Jesus himself being the chief cornerstone, thou art continually visiting it anew, giving it fresh light in its season of darkness, quickening it with new hope in times of fear, emancipating it from the thraldom of ignorance and superstition, and calling it forward into that bright realm where Christ maketh free. And as we bless thee above all for Him who came breathing upon us the fulness of thy love, the fulness of hope, the fulness of peace, so we thank thee for all reformers, apostles, confessors, and martyrs, in all times, in all parts of the world; and to-day we rejoice to bless thee for him whom thou didst inspire to be the advocate of peace, the friend of the oppressed, the deliverer of slaves, the benefactor of the poor, the teacher of children, the quickener of living souls, the emancipator from the bondage of priests.

We thank thee for the glorious affirmations which he hath given to us of the fatherhood of God, of our brotherhood in Christ, and of our heirship with him of a heaven of love, of light, and of liberty. We pray that this year a new impulse may be given to those blessed truths which were given us in charge by him who, though dead, still speaketh truths that shall speak in this land of his love,— the land for which he was willing to lay down his life.

We beseech thee, may thy ministering servants be aroused to new fidelity, having fresh motive, fresh hope, fresh courage; and may that Spirit which blessed some of us in our childhood, in the faithful pastor, the quickening friend, and the wise counsellor, with the spirit of reverence, of liberty, of love, of hope, and of holiness, be shed abroad through all our people's hearts, and make us one in the fellowship of the spirit, one in the hope of an immortality of love and joy and praise, and in the communion of the Holy Spirit; and may the benediction of that Spirit rest upon all that speak and all that hear to-day, in this assembly, and in many assemblies more throughout this land, and in other lands, hastening the time when the gospel of love and the gospel of unity and the gospel of hope shall triumph over all bitterness and darkness and fear and despair, and make us fellow-heirs with Christ of a glorious heaven. We ask it in that dear name unto which we commend ourselves, and all that is dear to us now and for evermore. *Amen.*

REMARKS OF REV. DR. PUTNAM (Chairman).

Friends, we bid you one and all a hearty welcome to this celebration of the one hundredth anniversary of the birthday of William Ellery Channing. Our first thought was to have a single service, to be held in this church, and to consist mainly of a commemorative discourse. But very soon the plan assumed a larger form, and especially as we remembered that here was a name that belonged to the Church universal, that was reverenced in all communions, and that would most fittingly be honored by friendly voices from all the churches and sects around us. We therefore arranged a more extensive programme, and cordially invited ministers and laymen of Brooklyn and elsewhere, of whatever creed or worship, if they had any sympathy with the spirit or purpose of the occasion, or had any word to speak of love or gratitude in memory of Channing, to come and freely participate in the services. We were very glad, nor were we at all surprised, to find that representative men of quite every faith or name in the community were ready and more than willing to respond to the call, and to lend their presence and voices, too, in furtherance of the object we had in view. Many of them are with us here, and you will have the pleasure of hearing what they have to offer. Others have expressed the deepest interest in the proposed meetings of the day, and regretted that absence from the city or pressing engagements would render it impossible for them to attend. We invite the freest utterance on the part of those who may feel moved to address the audience, be they Protestants or Catholics; and we expect here this morning, and at the Academy this evening, a full and varied expression of honest thought and feeling in relation to the one great theme that engages us.

I shall not long detain you with words of my own, since there are so many others whom you have come and are waiting to hear. But, before I take my seat, I must read two or three letters which, of the many I have received from far and near, to be read during the proceedings of the day, seem to me a fit introduction to what may follow at this particular meeting. The first is from Rev. William H. Channing, nephew and biographer of Dr. Channing, who, as you are well aware, has very recently arrived in this country from England, but whose engagement made long ago to be at Newport to-day prevents him from being present here with us. Another will be found to be of great interest to you, dictated as it was — though the signature is in his own handwriting — by the Rev. George G. Channing, of Milton, Mass., the only surviving brother of him whom we meet to honor, and himself now ninety-two years of age. Patiently he awaits the not-distant hour when he shall rise to join the ascended and sainted one. And another letter still is from the Rev. Charles T. Brooks, the revered and beloved poet-preacher, who for so many years was the minister of the Unitarian Church at Newport, Channing's birthplace.

[These letters, with many others, some of which were read by Rev. S. H. Camp at later stages of the meeting, and some were received after the celebration was over, will be found in the Appendix.]

I have a special purpose in introducing Mr. Brooks' letter just at this point. Much anxiety has been felt, as you know, lest the required sum of fifty thousand dollars for the new Memorial Church at Newport might not all be pledged by the time the corner-stone should be laid to-day. Great effort has been made to this end in various quarters. Last Saturday, I received a telegram from Rev. Mr. Schermerhorn, present minister of the Society there, saying that five thousand dollars more were needed, and asking additional help from the Church of the Saviour. On Monday, I sent him word that my people on Sunday had contributed another thousand, and asked him to let me know by Tuesday the state of things. This morning before breakfast, a telegram came, informing me that there was still, at the last hour, a deficiency of two thousand dollars. Through the generosity of a member of my parish, it was my privilege and joy to return immediately the message that the deficiency was met.

[Applause.] It is, therefore, permitted our assembled friends there to go on and lay the corner-stone of the new edifice with rejoicing; and I cannot help feeling a little pride that it has been given to my own beloved Church to add the capstone. [Renewed applause.]

And now I beg to present to you Rev. Dr. Farley, my venerable predecessor as pastor of this Church, who is connected by marriage with the family of Rev. George G. Channing, and who will speak to you of Dr. Channing from personal acquaintance and varied associations with him.

REMARKS OF REV. DR. F. A. FARLEY.

I do not think, my friends, that there is any heart among you that is filled with more grateful emotions than my own, in connection with all the associations of this anniversary. It was my good fortune — shall I not, rather, say that it was "by the blessing of God" my great privilege? — to know Dr. Channing in the early and more impressible period of my life, and especially during my preparatory studies for the ministry.

I recur to the time when I was a student in the Divinity School at Cambridge, and when I was accustomed to go into Boston on the return of the Lord's day, and listen to the preaching of this eminent man.

The first reminiscences of Dr. Channing, therefore, which come to my mind, are connected with his public ministry, with the discharge of his duties in the Christian pulpit; and I am sure that, among those who have been preachers of Christ and his holy gospel, never has there been a man who, from the sacred desk, more entirely held the minds and the hearts of those who listened to him; and never were there people who sat under preaching with more reverent and yet more tender feeling than those who heard the sweet, gentle, inspiring, mighty words of that sainted man of God.

After what was said by our dear Brother Peabody last evening in his admirable discourse, it might seem superfluous to attempt even to give expression to the recollections which rise from my own memory, in relation to the manner of Dr. Channing, the matter of his sermons, the power which they manifested, or even to glance at the influence which must have followed, and which we know did follow and is still destined to follow, his remarkable utterances and published writings. But I am called, and must obey.

Among the portraits of Channing there is one that has not been given to the public, and is now the property of my brother-in-law, George G. Channing, of Milton. It is a portrait painted by the celebrated Stuart of Boston. Somehow or other, the widow of Dr. Channing, and, I believe, both of his surviving children, did not value this portrait as it has always seemed to me it deserved; and therefore, among the various portraits which have been made, and which have been copied by the engraver and the photographer and sent forth to the world, this does not appear. But it remained a very treasured memory in the mind of the late Dr. Walter Channing, eminent in the medical profession, and of his brother George, as also of his sister, Mrs. Russell. It is now, as I said before, the property of the Milton branch of the family in Massachusetts. That portrait presents to my own remembrance Channing, as at that day he appeared in the pulpit of the old Federal Street Church. He is painted in the costume which was then almost universal with our clergy, of the robe and surplice and bands. And it brings him before me every time I look at it with a lifelike power, precisely as he seemed to me in the very prime of his active ministry. Next to that, I should place the portrait by S. Gambardella, painted in 1839, when Dr. Channing was fifty-nine years old; a fine line engraving of which, by Kimberly and Cheney, is prefixed to the second volume of the admirably finished Memoir of his distinguished uncle, by William Henry Channing; and a photograph of the same to our Brother Charles T. Brooks' interesting volume, "A Centennial Memory," just from the press, and which, in passing, I desire warmly to commend to my hearers.

The portrait before you was executed by the late Charles C. Ingham, of New York, at his own suggestion, on one of Channing's visits to that city, and is now the property of Dr. Bellows, who very kindly lent it to us for this occasion. In some respects, those of you who are familiar with the portrait of Gambardella will be able at once to trace a very considerable resemblance between this and that. Gambardella's is the latest, and was painted for Dr. Channing's intimate friend, the late Jonathan Phillips, of Boston, the senior deacon of his church. There is very much about Ingham's portrait that is like Dr. Channing in the later years of his life. It presents, certainly, an image of that thin, spare habit, which was a very marked point in his personal appearance, and of the *spirituelle* expression of his face.

You have been told that he was what, in a certain sense, may be called a tiny man. He *was* tiny in his figure. He was a very small man, and proportionately thin. I never knew him at any time when he appeared other than thin. From the loss of teeth in early life, his cheeks were comparatively hollow.

But there was that in his eye which, I am sure, my Brothers Peabody and Holland, and the few others who remember him, cannot forget. Not only did it speak and flash with his words in the pulpit; but in his private conversation and in his most familiar hours there was still, with all its softness and gentleness, a remarkably searching quality.

In regard to his pulpit ministrations, I beg to say that I have never heard a preacher in whom there was less of what might be called display. His manner was very simple and very engaging. He usually leaned upon his left arm, with his manuscript in the left hand; and this habit was largely, beyond doubt, the result of the delicacy of his constitution and general debility. A very slight movement — and always, as Dr. Peabody said last evening, purely "voluntary," with the forefinger of the right hand raised — was about all the gesture in which, ordinarily, he indulged. But most remarkable was his intonation. Why, although that voice from its general feebleness seemed to make it impossible that he should be heard, even in an auditorium of the size of the Federal Street Church, which was about the size of this, yet, such was its special and peculiar quality, that I suppose there never was a person who went out from those walls, after listening to Dr. Channing, without having heard and understood every word he uttered! One great reason of this may have been the intense silence which attended his public ministrations. The slightest foot-fall on the carpet could have been heard while he was speaking. At times, in his loftiest flights and in the most earnest appeals which he made to the hearts and consciences of his hearers, his voice was slightly raised; but there was no straining after effect. The manner was perfectly natural, just as natural as when he sat with you in conversation; and yet, impressive as it was, no one can describe it, and you are left entirely to your imagination to conceive of it.

But what shall I say of his prayers? There is one of our brethren now living, in very advanced age, of whom I have often heard it said — I refer to our venerable and beloved friend, Dr. Dewey — that it seemed to require a very painful effort to utter himself in public prayer. I think there never was a greater mistake. It was no effort, except it were simply the effort of self-control. So awed was he in the felt presence of the Almighty, and in the responsible office of leading the devotions of his people, that he seemed to speak under a certain, not morbid, but most natural feeling of constraint; and tears have been observed to follow his profound inward emotion. That the heart was full to the brim, every word that he uttered and the very expression of his countenance faithfully proved.

There was nothing in Dr. Channing of this peculiarity of Dr. Dewey. His prayers were the simplest utterances of the most affectionate and devout feeling of the confiding, trusting child, communing with an all-loving Father, uttered in the most tender and yet the most earnest tones. It became contagious, and lifted his hearers to the same plane of devout feeling with himself. All the words which he uttered in prayer seemed to come from the very depths of his own consciousness, and to reach those of his fellow-worshippers, who were thus brought at once into communion with the same Blessed Spirit who was filling his own heart. Taking these two men together, who were, moreover, most intimate friends, I think I never heard from other human lips such soul-subduing, touching, inspiring, uplifting prayer to the Source of all good.

I pass from Channing's public ministry to say a word or two of what I must esteem, as has been intimated already, a most blessed privilege,— that of personal communion with him in the quiet of his own study and home. I would go of an evening to his study, and, finding him alone, would sit with him, perhaps an hour or two; and I confess that the chief feeling which carried me there was the consciousness of the merest pupil in the presence of a great teacher. Shall I say that he commanded me into this feeling? By no means.

From the reverence which was inspired by what I had experienced of his work in public, and from the knowledge of his saintly character derived through what afterwards became a dear family connection, I realized to some extent in what a remarkable presence I stood, and what a fulness there was in the fountain within him, of the sprinklings of which I desired to partake.

I see in many notices of Dr. Channing references to him as a remarkable conversationalist. I remember very well one occasion, after his brother-in-law, Mr. Allston, had received a letter from Coleridge, in which allusion was made to him, I asked Dr. Channing who he considered the best conversationalist that he met abroad, the two prominent names at that time being Sir James Mackintosh and Coleridge. He very promptly answered, "Sir James Mackintosh." He added that Mackintosh had remarkable conversational power, and that it was *truly* conversational; while Coleridge, on the other hand, discoursed, and that one had only to propose to Coleridge a subject or a question to have him instantly pour forth from his rich and cultured mind and soul most remarkable utterances, quite at length. I could not help thinking, at the moment, that that was, to a certain extent, the case with himself. So far as my own experience was concerned, it really seemed so to me; but then you must remember I was only a novice, an inexperienced young man. And I regard it as a blessed condescension on his part that, when I ventured to bring a subject before him, he gave me such distinct and prolonged attention, and shed upon it such a flood of light.

In the letter referred to, Coleridge said, in substance, "I have had the pleasure of becoming acquainted with your honored friend, Dr. Channing, whom I consider the most remarkable conversationalist that I ever met from your land." When I repeated this, he said, with his quietest manner and gentlest voice, albeit with a slight twinkle of his eye, "Ah! that was because I was so good a listener."

When I was in his study, at various times, I find on recollection that he was accustomed, as we used to say in college, to "pump" me. He began by questioning me, I might almost say, in the Socratic way; but his object seemed to be to get into my mind,—a very easy thing for him to do, by the way, for there was very little there at that time, at least; and, by the questions and the themes which he proposed to riddle me through and through; and then, by and by, to help me, in the kindest manner possible, at once to realize my own faulty way of search, and put me on the right track, by pouring into my soul some of those effective and weighty suggestions which so frequently fell from his lips. Such was his way of dealing with a young man, and was it not a wholesome way?

I would come from him to the family of my wife, tell them where I had been, and express my delight in the visit. They wondered why. And here I am led to speak of Channing as he appeared in his ordinary intercourse. Persons of high culture and intellectual accomplishment met him, not exactly with awe, but with a feeling of profound respect and even reverence; and others, with entire confidence, so that they could be at once at ease with him; while there were many cases in his congregation, as in that very family to which I have alluded, where the moment he appeared among them there was shrinking as from a being of a superior order.

Now was this because he put on airs? Was it because he assumed anything? Why, he was the simplest of human beings in his whole manner and speech. But it was the intense reverence, notwithstanding all the admiration which they might have of him as a preacher and as a man, which he inspired through the saintliness of his very bearing and life on all occasions and under all circumstances; and they could not forget it.

I would say, "I have had a most delightful evening with Dr. Channing." "Delightful? How could it have been delightful? Why, I shrink into nothingness when I am in his presence," would be the response, perhaps. And then I told them that I went there and got just what I wanted; that in the veriest sweetness of condescension he listened to my poor words, and poured out the better words and the richer thoughts he had to give me, and sent me away from that place again and again with the inspiration I had gained quickening my resolves for good, and filling me with a heartier thirst for truth, knowledge, and freedom. I could not possibly make it understood that to me, in the relation in which I stood to him as a very humble and a very desirous-of-learning pupil, it was possible that I had had a delightful evening.

How often have I heard him lament that he could not draw all his people nearer to him in more familiar intercourse in his pastoral walk, — in which no one could have been more faithful, — and divest them of all timidity in their approaches! His sympathy in their sorrows and trials, however, all felt; for the spell of that none could resist. He had no "small talk"; but he was simple and gentle as a child. And this leads me to allude to his love of children and his manner toward them. Never can I forget a little incident in connection with one of my own. I had taken my oldest boy, then perhaps four or five years old, to spend a night at "Oakland," his lovely summer retreat at Portsmouth, R.I. His marked kindness soon won the heart of the little fellow; and the next day, after early lunch preparatory to our drive home, and the chaise being ready at the gate, the doctor took the child, nothing loath, in his arms, and, carrying him to the vehicle, put him safely in, kissed him, and bade him "good-by."

I was about to say something of the charm of this remarkable man in his home at Rhode Island, which I had so often the happiness of enjoying during my first ministry at Providence. It was one of the loveliest spots in the world; but his presence, sweet yet dignified manners, affectionate intercourse with his family and guests, only made it the more lovely. "Happy," says his nephew in his "Memoir," — "happy the guest who is to ride with Dr. Channing in his chaise! It is a most plain vehicle, indeed, and the horse knows well that he may trespass almost without remonstrance on his master's good-nature; but who can regret the slowness of a drive which prolongs the delight of his conversation?" Happy, indeed! On one of these drives, when he had just been reading a spirited paper by Samuel J. May, advocating the extremest doctrine of non-resistance, the doctor, after analyzing the argument of our excellent friend, raised his tiny but clenched fist, — at the moment and under the circumstances seeming almost ludicrously small, — and, turning to me, exclaimed, "Ah, Brother Farley, but there are occasions when we *must* fight!" But I leave this theme, so much fuller and better treated than I can pretend to treat it, to the delightful pages of his nephew and Mr. Brooks.

There are two occasions in my life, Mr. President, which brought me into close and most affecting contact with Dr. Channing, which can never be forgotten, and the remembrance and influence of which will go with me, I trust, to my final account. To him, indeed, more than to any other mere man, more than to any other being that has trod this earth, except my divine Saviour, do I owe whatever of quickening impulse I have felt in my religious, moral, professional life. The first of these was my ordination to the Christian ministry at Providence, in 1828, when he preached that great sermon on "Likeness to God." With all who then heard him, despite the emotion which naturally thrilled a young heart at such a time, I was carried away from myself. Never, too, was his manner so inspired and grand, so animated and free; and this was the universal judgment on all sides expressed. By accident, the platform on which he stood lifted his tiny form so much above the pulpit cushion that he could not, as was his wont, lean upon it. When he began to speak, he seemed slightly embarrassed, and now and then looked around and beneath him, as though he sought relief; but then, gathering up his strength in his decision to go on, he stood erect, and went through with his discourse with the unction and fervid eloquence of a prophet. Then came the good old symbolic custom of the Congregational Churches, which seems to have well-nigh died out in our branch of that body,— "the laying on of hands"; and he, with others of the fathers and brethren in the ministry, laid his hand upon my head. If anything could have added to the touching and solemn significance of those ordination services, it was the conscious pressure of that hand upon my head, while the prayer of consecration rose in my behalf to the Father of our spirits.

Once more, he it was — in connection with his colleague, of blessed memory, my very dear friend in later years, Ezra Stiles Gannett — who with his own hands joined my wife's hands and mine in the holy sacrament of marriage; and his look and word as he gave us his blessing went, I tell you, to the heart.

Do you wonder, as I close, that I look back on my intercourse with that beloved and saintly man with feelings impossible indeed to express, and which I must leave you to imagine? With unfeigned gratitude, with great joy in the remembrance; and with confident faith that if his spirit be conscious now of what we and so many all over Christendom are engaged in to-day, he joins in our thanksgivings for what he was inspired to do, and the fruits of which we are reaping, for the Church Universal, and its "unity of spirit in the bond of peace"; yet, let us give the glory to God! [Applause.]

Dr. Farley's address was listened to with deep interest by the audience. At its conclusion, the Chairman introduced, as the next speaker, Rev. J. B. Thomas, D.D., Pastor of the Pierrepont Street Baptist Church, who was heartily applauded, as he came forward to the platform.

REMARKS OF REV. J. B. THOMAS, D.D.

Were there no other occasion, I should be most happy to be here to-day in response to the courtesy of my valued friend and neighbor, whose spotless life and faithful ministry and amiable spirit I have so long known. I find it easy to obey the Scripture precept to love my neighbor as myself; and I am glad to share in all things that make him glad and in all things that he reverences.

But, aside from that, this occasion has for me an interest, as I trust it has for all lovers of their kind, who believe that good men are not superfluous in the world, and are not to be hastily forgotten.

I am associated with that body of people whom Dean Stanley recently called "the austere sect," — the Baptists, — and whom he regards, and probably many others regard, as the most unprogressive Christian people. It might seem strange that there should be the suggestion of any possible affinity between them and you who are accounted the most progressive; and yet, were I to look to-day for the largest and most trenchant compilation of authorities sustaining our views on the particular question which outwardly separates us from other Christians, I should look for it in the Racovian Catechism.

If you and Dr. Channing are the product of the Reformation, so are we. If you insist upon the spirit of free inquiry, so did we. If you insist upon supremacy of the spirit over form, whether in organization or in expression, so have we, so *do* we. The root of our organization is not in exterior separation, by ordinance or by creed, but in the radical proposition that the word of God alone, unmanacled, unperverted by the decree or the organized influence of man, is sufficient for the individual soul. Such is the corner-stone of our organization.

When I say this, I do not forget that, in the years since the Racovian Catechism was promulgated, you and we have gone far apart. I have no fear to-day that you will be mistaken for Baptists because you invite me to speak, or that I shall be mistaken for a Unitarian because I respond to your invitation.

I am reminded, however, that this occasion is a memorial, not of the particular faith which you hold or of the particular organization which you represent, but of the particular man to whom you do honor. I am reminded that that man himself accounted himself, and I trust that by those who appreciate him he is accounted, as above the organizations which he deprecated as merely provisional, regarding them as matters of necessity, but believing that man was before the organized church, that he will be after it, and that he is superior to it. [Applause.] I remember with what earnestness he inveighed and protested against those barriers and hinderances which cramped from without, rather than developed from within, the nature that God has given us. I remember how sterling a champion he was for freedom to seek the truth; and, if you will pardon me, still more by his spirit than by his word, a champion of the purest spirituality in religion.

Many years have passed since he was taken from us. In

that very profound and moving discourse to which I had the felicity of listening with many of you last night, the question was asked, How has the time so changed that men of all faiths are ready to do reverence to Dr. Channing? It is true, unquestionably, that the time has gone by when men will be at once disposed of by classifying them under the organizations to which they belong. Men count as *men*. *Ponderantur non numerantur*. In parliamentary assemblies, sometimes, in haste, they read bills by their titles, and so dispose of them; but let men no longer be read by their titles or by their ecclesiastical relationships: let them be pondered, in order that we may know what is in them. No man was ever more earnest than Dr. Channing in the opinion that the principal thing in a man is not the specific intellectual conception of truth that he has, but his devotion to the truth *as* truth; that a man should be true to the truth,—not that he should accept my opinion or your opinion, but that he should maintain his own opinion until he get a better one, and that he should be seeking always for a better one. This, I apprehend, he put above any exterior relation. This, I take it, he thought would bring the world along, rather than any mechanical process. This, as I understand it, he believed to be God's ideal of, and God's preparation for, the progress of truth and of Christianity in the world. And this I sympathize with.

I remember Dr. Channing's trenchant papers on creeds, copies of which I see here. Dr. Channing was an alert disputant. He was a man of rare clearness in statement. He was a man of vigorous and forcible logical faculty, and, I think, not altogether unwilling to cross the sword in debate,— for men like to do that which they can do well; and yet I have never been prepared to accept the suggestion that his discussions were emotionless, and transparent only because they were icy. They rather seem to me to be luminous with the light within the cloud. As has been pithily said of another: "His words are vascular. Cut them, and they would bleed." Underneath them, you catch the throb of the heart; and this it is that will perpetuate his memory among all men. Men's thoughts perish in the day that they are born, they are but as the leaves of autumn; but the spirit that informs them lives in them and goes beyond them, as it goes beyond the life of man.

In that noble discussion of last evening, emphasis was laid upon Dr. Channing's loyalty to Christ. "Grace be with all them that love our Lord Jesus Christ in sincerity." I was taught it in my childhood, I seek to apprehend it in my manhood. May God let me die with that spirit in my heart and those words upon my lips.

When Dr. J. W. Alexander died, and the passage was quoted, "I know whom I believed," and it was corrected by inserting the preposition "*in*," he said, "No! no! I know *whom* I have believed." Now, Dr. Channing did not profess to know all about Him whom he believed: he did profess to know Him. As through his clear eye he looked beneath the husk of things in politics, in humanitarian reform, in the discussions of the time, in literature, in all the phases of human existence, and saw life within form greater than form, so he reverenced Christ as revealed through a deeper faculty and a more spiritual intimacy than logical definition brings. Therefore, he was a man of mighty power in his day, and a man whose influence will not speedily die.

I should perhaps stop here, for I am not a missionary to this people; but will you permit me, having expressed, as I sincerely feel, the most unfeigned admiration for Dr. Channing, to make a suggestion, which I would not have ventured but for an allusion that I heard from one [Dr. Peabody] whom men of all faiths reverence, and to whose utterances they listen with devout respect, and with the most earnest desire to profit by them? Alluding to the widely diverse developments of Unitarianism since Dr. Channing's day, he spoke of it as the "Texas of Christendom," to which men holding all shades of opinion had resorted, when forced by the rigor of creeds to leave their denominational relations. Accepting the figure, the inquiry is suggested, "How comes Texas to be so proverbial a refuge as to make the allusion significant?" Was it not that, lying between the United States and Mexico, it suffered the inconveniences and dangers of the frontier, being open to emigration from either side? Dr. Channing himself expressed great apprehensions, as we are reminded, in regard to its annexation to the Union, lest the Union should be itself deteriorated.

His apprehensions were in some measure realized, but yet were perhaps exaggerated so far as their ultimate results are concerned; for, although Texas did get into the Union somewhat modified, it has not destroyed the Union, and it has a future yet before it.

Allusion was made to the transcendental element which affected theology in New England. If I remember rightly, there was a sentence of Dr. Channing's in one of his articles to this purport: That all sects, all bodies of people, have tried too much to define their religion; that the Infinite is undefinable, and inaccessible to the square, the compass, and the measuring lines of logic; that transcendentalism which is intellectual is but a counterfeit and a mockery. It is the cloud without the glory, thin, cold, and life-destroying.

But there is a transcendentalism that reaches to the Throne. There is a transcendentalism in which life grows and thrives, and in which Dr. Channing himself was perpetually bathed. The dangers of scholasticism, and the damage it has done, he did not overestimate; but will you permit me to say that in his discussions, it seems to me, he may have opened a narrow gap at least toward the scholastic method, in meeting subtlety by subtlety in the attempt at an intellectual counter-definition of the Divine? The old ecclesiastical enginery, the dungeon-houses, the instruments of torture, might perhaps better have been burned up by the fires of love than hammered down by catapults of polemic discussion.

But, my friends, let me say this,— and pardon me for having detained you so long,— while I do not accept Dr. Channing's theology so far as formal statements are concerned, and while I am not therefore a Unitarian, I bow humbly at the feet of the man whom I believe to have been a brave, pure, devout, unselfish worshipper and disciple of the Master that I serve; and I greet you in memory of the hour in which he was born; and I pray God that, as the years go on, the clash of war and the strife of tongues, and all those divisions that make Christianity to mean anarchy rather than a kingdom, may be overcome, and that the shadows may flee before the better dawn which brings the better day, in which distant things shall be seen to be distant and immeasurable, in which friends shall not be mistaken for enemies, nor enemies for friends. [Applause.]

The CHAIRMAN. — That was a voice from out the great Baptist communion, expressive of the very spirit of Roger Williams. And now I have the pleasure of introducing to you, from another large and powerful denomination which has done much good in the world, which has had great success in the past, and which we hope may have still greater success in the future, the Rev. Dr. Buckley of the Hanson Place Methodist Church of this city, who has just arrived, and will say some words to you.

REMARKS OF REV. DR. J. M. BUCKLEY.

Mr. Chairman, and Ladies and Gentlemen,— I am not doctrinally or theologically in any sense in sympathy with what are distinctively called Unitarian views. The gentlemen who invited me to speak here informed me that I would be permitted to express my candid estimate of the life and work of the Rev. William Ellery Channing; and I have assumed that it is possible to do that in a manner that shall be in harmony with the spirit of this occasion.

The few moments that I shall speak will be devoted to that simple statement. Invited at a late hour, I should not have presumed myself competent to make such a statement if I had not, ever since I entered the ministry, carefully read and studied the works of Dr. Channing. I had the fortune to begin my ministry in the State of New Hampshire and the town of Exeter, the site of Phillips Academy, within a very few miles of Portsmouth, where at that time the Rev. Dr. Peabody was an honored pastor. The system to which I belong rarely trusts a minister, in his earlier stages, very long in one place. Consequently, after having had the opportunity to derive all the good I could from the people of Exeter, and to communicate all it was supposed possible that I could give, I was removed to Dover; but I was still as near Portsmouth as before.

Now, Dr. Peabody I heard preach with profound respect; and I was led to believe, when I heard him, that the difference between his theological views and mine was very slight. But when I removed to Dover, where there was a very large church of the Unitarian denomination, I found the incumbent of that church a very different man theologically, to say no more, from the Rev. Dr. Peabody. And when he and I met on the School Board,— both of us being appointed as members of that Board, according to the custom which prevails in that city, — while we devoted considerable time to the consideration of matters of education, as required at our hands by the law, in the intervals we devoted a great deal more time to theological debate; and I found that the difference between him and me was so vast as to be absolutely irreconcilable. In order to prepare myself to convince him that he had widely departed from the doctrines of the Unitarian fathers, I procured the works of Dr. Channing, and during the two years I spent there I always managed to have a quotation ready for him. The quotations that seemed to disturb him most were those in which Dr. Channing stated that the death of Christ appeared to have some peculiar and special relation to the pardon of sin. I was familiar with those passages. I could repeat them; and I assure you it gave me a great deal of pleasure to remind my radical friend of those words of Dr. Channing. And while I was studying Dr. Channing, even from that somewhat equivocal point of view, I came to love his style very much, — not the less so because I saw from the beginning that I should never be able to imitate its clearness, its beauty, or its marvellous balance.

Now, I do not know who is in this house; but I fancy to myself that we have in the city of Brooklyn a clergyman whose style in very many particulars resembles that of Dr. Channing. I refer to the Rev. Dr. Storrs. I say in *many particulars*. I do not for a moment suppose the resemblance to be perfect; but in the particular of the marvellous capacity to illustrate thought, and to balance every part, and to construct a discourse so that it shall resemble a symmetrical piece of architecture, I think I see a very great similarity. I may be permitted to say that I think in simplicity Dr. Channing surpassed the gentleman to whom I refer, and almost every great speaker in the country to-day. I do not suppose that Dr. Channing as a public speaker would have attracted great attention in the South, from his lack of a certain kind of fervency, or in the West, from his excess, relatively to the attainments in that region, of refinement; but in New England, and in the more cultivated circles of the Middle States, it seems to me Dr. Channing's style was exactly adapted to make the profoundest impression. I have never supposed that he was a logician, in the technical sense of that term. I think it would have been impossible for John Calvin and Dr. Channing to converse together to their mutual satisfaction and edification, entirely apart from their doctrinal views. I believe that John Wesley would have considered Dr. Channing a genuine Christian, but that he would not have been able to argue with him. John Wesley was a dialectician and a logician, who used his logic as a means to an end, to prove the point he had in view at the time. Dr. Channing — and, in order to assure you that I have not been drawn astray in my former reflections, I will say that I have spent a couple of hours this morning in reading his selected discourses — seems to me to have been a philosopher. He was, however, led aside by a poetic tendency from the straight lines of philosophy; and it appears to me that he was not as logically consistent as some who would go further.

Permit me a single word here. If I adopted the root principles of Dr. Channing himself, I fancy that my temperament, my thoughts, and my way of following out to the last results what I seemed to myself to see, would take me a great deal further than he went. On the other hand, if I had such a pure spirituality, if I may use such a term, as that which he possessed, but which I lay no claim to by nature,—and I say nothing in this presence about grace!— I fancy that my temperament would not lead me to go so far as he did, but would lead me rather to content myself with dwelling in the regions of experience.

Dr. Channing was of very great use to the Methodists in

the following manner. He used the splendor of his intellect against Calvinism. In that respect, he was of very great benefit to us. Our entrance into New England was under peculiar circumstances. Our first preacher stood on Boston Common and lifted up his voice. No church was opened to receive him in the State of Massachusetts. He lifted up his voice in song. He understood then what the world understands now,— that the people will hear a singer when they will not hear a speaker. Though he had but few listeners to begin with, his powerful voice, singing in a style that was not known in that part of the country, soon attracted a vast concourse. He lifted up his voice like a trumpet to denounce Calvinism; and certainly a man is more sure when he is in a dogmatic state of a satisfactory flow of speech than when he depends upon the changing moods of feeling. And he created a great excitement; and, when he waked the people up to understand what he was doing, an old gentleman came forward, and, with a voice as loud as that of the speaker, said, "Are we to stand on Boston Common and hear our foundation principles attacked?" They all agreed they were not there for that purpose; and, as in the case of Paul on Mars Hill, some said they would hear him again, and others said, "What doth this babbler say?"

Such was our entrance into New England, and we could not do much for a long time; but Dr. Channing used the splendor of his intellect and his marvellous influence, and fought our battles, so far as Calvinism was concerned.

Now, Mr. Chairman, if, in the complacency which is a part of our denominational life, growing out of our great success, we felicitate ourselves on having the sense and grace to stop a little this side of Dr. Channing's final point, we should not be blamed for that. We appreciate the work he did in assisting us in our protest against Calvinism. And if he were alive to-day, and were to apply for admission into our church as a layman, I, standing here as a warrior upon the walls of Zion, would vote for the admission of a man of God, a patriot, a philanthropist, a friend of temperance, a friend of his country, a friend of the laboring classes, and a friend of all good men; but candor requires me to say that, if he were to apply for admission into our ministry, while I should rejoice to recognize him as a friend of humanity, and, I will say with Brother Thomas, as a friend of our Lord Jesus Christ, and as one whose influence in many particulars has promoted the interests of the kingdom of Christ in the world, especially in this country, I am afraid, sir, that logical consistency would compel me to raise some points, the final effect of which might be to delay or embarrass his entrance into the ministry.

This, Mr. Chairman, is my candid opinion of the life and work of Dr. Channing. I rejoice that he has lived. I acknowledge my indebtedness to him. I do not positively know that even, from my point of view, his influence has been deleterious to the progress of Christ's kingdom in the world. But his principles were not mine. I cannot accept his views; and therefore I simply would honor him as a great factor in American civilization, and believe that every citizen of the United States, in making a list of the men of influence and of power that our country has produced, is compelled, with delight and admiration, to include among the foremost the name of William Ellery Channing. [Applause.]

Ladies and gentlemen, I am very much obliged to you for the opportunity of speaking to-day, and for the attention which you have given me.

The CHAIRMAN.— We are glad, you see, to have the freest utterances of members of different communions. We propose to have the greatest possible variety. And so, having heard from our friend Dr. Thomas, of the Baptist Church, and our friend Dr. Buckley, of the Methodist Church, not to take too large a leap at once, I will call upon our friend Mr. Chadwick to offer some remarks and read us his Centennial Ode.

REMARKS OF REV. J. W. CHADWICK.

Ladies and Gentlemen,— You are well aware, no doubt, that, in making the preparations for this noble and beautiful occasion, Dr. Putnam has said to one man, "Go," and he goeth, and to another, "Come," and he cometh, and to a third, "Do this," and he doeth it; and, when he said to me, "Go you and couch the words you have to say in a sort of rhyme and rhythm," I did just as he told me. But for Dr. Putnam's commands, I should not presume to vary from my ordinary form of speech; but, as it is, I am to read to you a kind of hymn, or ode, on The Hundredth Anniversary of Channing's Birthday:—

CENTENNIAL ODE.

A hundred years ago to-day!
   How often in this latter time,
   In fond memorial speech or rhyme,
Has it been ours these words to say!

A hundred years to-day, we said,
   Since Concord bridge and Lexington
   Saw the great struggle well begun
And the first heroes lying dead.

A hundred years since Bunker Hill
   Saw the red-coated foemen reel
   Once and again before the steel
Of Prescott's men, victorious still

In their defeat; a hundred years
   Since Independence-bell rang out
   To all the people round about,
Who answered it with deafening cheers,

Proclaiming, spite the scorner's scorn,
    That then and there — the womb of time
    Through sufferance triumphing sublime —
Another nation had been born.

"All men are equal in their birth,"
    Rang out the steeple-rocking bell;
    Rejoice, O heaven! Give heed, O hell!
Here *was* good news to all the earth.

And still our hearts have kept the count
    Of things that daily brought more near,
    Through various hap of hope or fear,
The pattern visioned in the mount.

Nor yet the tale is fully told
    Of all the years that brought us pain,
    And through the age of iron again
The dawning of the age of gold.

But naught of this has brought us here,
    With the old saying on our lips,
    What time the rolling planet dips
Into the spring-tide of the year.

Apart from all the dire alarms
    Of field or flood in that old time,
    With reverent feet our fancies climb
To where a mother's circling arms

Enraptured hold a babe new born;
    And who was there to prophesy,
    Though loving hearts beat strong and high,
Of what a day this was the morn?

For in that life but just begun
    The prescient fates a gift had bound
    As dear to man as any found
Within the courses of the sun, —

A gift of manhood strong and wise,
    Nor foreign to the lowliest earth —
    Whereon the Word has human birth —
Howe'er conversant with the skies.

A hundred years ago to-day
    Since Channing's individual life
    From out the depths of being, rife
With spiritual essence, found a way,

And welcome here, and forces kind
   To gently nurse his growing power
   With steady help until the flower
Of instinct was a conscious mind.

To him the sea its message brought,
   Filling his mind with sacred awe
   What time his eye enraptured saw
Its wildest tumult; or he caught

From its deep calm some peace of heart;
   To him the ages brought their lore
   Of books, and living men their store
Of thought, and still the better part

Of all his nurture was the eye
   Turned inward, seeking in the mind
   Some higher, deeper law to find
Than that which spheres the starry sky.

And so the youth to manhood came,
   A being frail — with nameless eyes,
   That seemed to look on Paradise —
As clear as dew, as clean as flame.

He willed in quiet to abide,
   Leading his flock through pastures green
   And by the waters still, where lean
The mystic trees on either side.

But on his listening ear there fell
   The jarring discord of the sects,
   Still making with their war of texts
The pleasant earth a kind of hell.

He saw the Father's sacred name
   Made dim by Calvary's suffering rood;
   Man devil-born — a spawning flood,
Engendering naught but curse and shame.

He saw the freedom of the mind
   Denied, and doubt esteemed a crime; —
   The path whereby the boldest climb
To heights which cowards never find.

He saw the manhood which to him
   Was image of the highest God
   Trodden as if it were a clod
'Neath Slavery's idol-chariot grim.

He saw it fouled with various sin,
    Sick'ning from lack of air and light,
    Abjuring glories infinite
To fatten at the sensual bin.

He heard and saw; his shepherd's rod
    With grieving heart he broke in twain;
    The wondering world beheld again
A prophet of the living God.

Then, as of old, was heard a voice:
    "His way prepare," and "Come with me,
    All ye that heavy-laden be,
Take up my burden, and rejoice."

It rang through all the sleepy land
    In tones so sweet and silver clear
    The waking people seemed to hear
The accents of divine command.

The statesman heard it in his place,
    The oppressor in his cursed field,
    And hearts beyond the ocean yield
Allegiance to his truth and grace.

Our Father, God; our Brother, Man:
    On these commandments twain he hung
    The law and prophets all, and rung
For all the churches' eager ban

A hundred changes deep and strong;
    Let who would hear him or forbear,
    The ancient lie he would not spare,
The doubtful right, the vested wrong.

What words were his of purest flame
    When, straining up from height to height,
    He felt the Presence infinite
And named the Everlasting Name!

With him the thought and deed were one:
    Man was indeed the Son of God;
    "What, strike a man!"* Break every rod
Of hate beneath the all-seeing sun!

So greatly born, how dare to trail
    Our festal garlands in the mire!
    How dare not evermore aspire
To Him who is within the veil!

---

* His argument against flogging in the Navy.

In weakness made each day more strong,
   Softly his days went trooping past
   Till, robed in beauty, came the last,
And with the sun he went along;

Not to oblivion's dreamless sleep,
   But, like the sun, on other lands
   To shine, where other, busier hands
The fields immortal sow and reap.

And he is ours! Yes, if we dare,
   Leaving the letter of his creed,
   Say to his mighty spirit, "Lead,
We follow hard." Yes, if no care

Is ours for aught but this: to know
   What is God's truth, and knowing this
   To count it still our dearest bliss
To go with that where'er it go.

So shall we go with him; so feel
   That comfort which the Spirit of Truth
   Gives all who with his loving ruth
Are pledged to her for woe or weal.

O thou whom, though we have not seen,
   We love! Upon our toilsome way
   Be thy pure spirit as a ray
From out that Light which is too clean

Uncleanness to behold; shine clear,
   That to our dimly peering eyes
   All hidden truths, all specious lies,
That which they are may straight appear.

There is no ending to thy road,
   No limit to thy fleeting goal,
   But speeds the ever-greatening soul
From truth to truth, from God to God.

[Applause.]

The CHAIRMAN.— Mr. Oliver Johnson was in the earliest fight with William Lloyd Garrison against slavery, and we deem ourselves fortunate to have him here this morning; for he knows something about Dr. Channing's connection with that movement, and had the great pleasure and privilege of listening to some of Dr. Channing's famous public discourses, as published in his works. Mr. Johnson will now address you.

REMARKS OF MR. OLIVER JOHNSON.

Mr. JOHNSON.— I feel myself very highly honored in being invited to say a few words on this occasion. I have the greatest reverence for the memory of Channing. My acquaintance with him was indeed but slight. When I went to Boston, as a boy, in 1830, I used often to see him in the street. His figure was familiar to me; but that was the time as you all remember — or at least as you all *know*, if you are not old enough to remember — when the great controversy between Orthodoxy and Unitarianism in Boston was at its height,— Dr. Beecher the great leader of Orthodoxy, and Dr. Channing the great leader of Unitarianism. I was then an intensely earnest orthodox man. I had united with the church a few years before, and was looking forward to the Christian ministry; and I was told by those around me, in whom I had the utmost confidence, that Unitarianism was infidelity, or something not much better than that. Therefore, when I first came in contact with Dr. Channing, I was under the influence of very strong prejudice,— not against him personally, however, except as he was the representative of Unitarianism.

It was not a great while after this that the first Antislavery Society — the parent of all that great circle of associations which agitated this land nearly fifty years ago, and which prepared the way for the abolition of slavery in our country — was organized in Boston; and, in the preliminary meetings which we held to consider the question of organizing that society, I met the noble man [Samuel E. Sewall] whose letter has just been read, then one of the young men of Channing's congregation; and I said to myself, "Now I shall see what Unitarianism is." I never shall forget the strong prejudice with which I came in contact with that young man, and with another equally noble, Mr. Ellis Gray Loring, also a member of Dr. Channing's congregation. I expected to find those men destitute of a Christian spirit. I supposed I should hear, when they opened their lips, some utterance of infidelity. I believed with all my heart that figs could not grow upon thistles; and, as I had been told that Unitarianism was a thistle, I was looking out for something very bad to come from these men. But, when I witnessed their Christian deportment and their firm attachment to the truth, I felt rebuked for my presumption; and I began to open my eyes, and to ask whether, after all, I had not been misinformed, and whether it was not possible for a good man to come up under the influence of Unitarianism. And let me say that I was not long in correcting the error into which I had fallen. In the Christian character of those two men was revealed to me the spirit of Channing and of Unitarianism.

It was my privilege to hear Channing preach but once, and then I listened with orthodox ears. It was on the occasion of the delivery of his "Election Sermon" in 1832, which will be found in his works under the title of "Spiritual Freedom." It is certainly one of the finest of his discourses. He addressed the "assembled wisdom" of the Commonwealth in that historic place, the Old South Church. I recall the scene now as freshly as if it were only yesterday that it occurred. As he spake, he held his manuscript in his left hand, and his voice, though gentle as a woman's, filled the house. How vividly I recall his utterance of this striking passage, which will live while the English language continues to be spoken! —

I call that mind free which jealously guards its intellectual rights and powers, which calls no man master, which does not content itself with a passive or hereditary faith, which opens itself to light whencesoever it may come, which receives new truth as an angel from heaven, which, while consulting others, inquires still more of the oracle within itself, and uses instructions from abroad, not to supersede, but to quicken and exalt its own energies.

The exquisite intonation and emphasis with which this and other passages of the discourse were read made a deep impression upon my youthful mind.

Dr. Channing at first kept aloof from the abolitionists, partly because of the intense individualism which led him to distrust all organized movements, and partly because our bold and uncompromising utterances grated harshly upon his sensitive — may I not say his over-sensitive? — ear. He could not well bear the noise of the ecclesiastical machinery by means of which his own religious thoughts were sent forth to the world. He shrank from being called an abolitionist, partly from the same feeling which led him to say, "I have little or no interest in the Unitarians as a sect; I have hardly anything to do with them; I can endure no sectarian bonds." He stood for himself in all things. The abolitionists were exceedingly unpopular; and he probably thought he should gain a more favorable hearing if he magnified somewhat the differences between them and himself. But he did not by this means escape the brand of abolitionist. The whole pro-slavery party stamped it upon him, hurling at his head every epithet that they had bestowed upon Garrison. The good doctor, notwithstanding his clear moral insight, was slow in accepting the doctrine of immediate emancipation. He was not quite sure that it would be safe to set all the slaves free at once. The results of emancipation in the British West Indies convinced him at last, as his Lenox address proves. He thought that a great sin did not necessarily imply great sinners, and he had somehow persuaded himself that there was a way of touching off an anti-slavery gun, and a well-loaded one too, "aisily," as the Irishman said, without making a disturbance. Experience soon corrected this mistake on his part. The reverberations of his own gun, so gently discharged as he thought, startled thousands from their sleep, and made the slave-holders and their apologists angry. The abolitionists, it must be confessed, did not relish his criticisms, and paid him back in his own coin. The account was long ago settled; and they have no unpleasant memories, but are glad to honor him for his noble and timely testimony. His agreements with them were central and vital, his differences but incidental and transient. Nor should it be forgotten that he bore with meekness a load of reproach, such as fell to the lot only of the bravest and truest champions of the slave. Even in his own parish, his message was unheeded, save by a few. When he asked that the doors of his church might be opened for a eulogy upon his beloved friend, Dr. Follen, a warm-hearted abolitionist, to be pronounced by another dear friend, the late Samuel J. May, they were rudely shut in his face. In this and many other ways, he was made to feel that his testimony against slavery had greatly impaired his reputation. But he neither wavered nor turned back. His voice grew clearer and stronger to the end.

When in 1837 Elijah P. Lovejoy was murdered at Alton, and the liberty of the press struck down by violence, Channing was the first man in Boston to seek to bring the people of that city to a sense of the importance of speaking out against that outrage. It was through his influence that a great meeting was held in Faneuil Hall, and held — let me say it to the shame of Boston — in the daytime, because we dared not hold it in the evening, knowing that it would be broken up by a mob. His friend Jonathan Phillips, the senior deacon of his church, took the chair. I shall never forget the appearance of Dr. Channing as he presented himself in that meeting. His face was all aglow with solemn earnestness, his voice tremulous with emotion, his whole attitude and bearing that of a prophet with a message from God. He spoke briefly, but eloquently. There followed him into that meeting a distinguished lawyer of Boston, a member of his own congregation, James T. Austin, Esq., who sprang to his feet the moment the doctor's speech was concluded, and, intruding himself upon the audience, uttered a most disgraceful harangue, which he doubtless thought would have the effect of breaking up the meeting. For a time there seemed to be reason to fear that he would succeed in his purpose; but, under the inspiring eloquence of Phillips, all such apprehensions were soon averted. The voice of that meeting went forth to cheer the friends of freedom all over the land.

Once, and once only, did I have a personal interview with Channing; but that to me was memorable. It was at his home in Portsmouth, near Newport, in 1838 or 1839. I was then the secretary and general agent of the Rhode Island Anti-slavery Society, and I eagerly embraced an opportunity to visit him. He received me with a gracious sweetness and dignity that I shall never forget, and his counsel, modestly given, was most cheering and helpful. In that day, the anti-slavery lecturer was often called to face a mob. More than once had the tar-kettle been heated for me, and the garment of feathers woven for my behoof. In such circumstances, the words of Channing gave me fresh courage.

There are not many persons, if there is even a single one, in this house, who, like myself, witnessed the funeral rites of Channing, and looked upon his placid, I had almost said his seraphic, face in death. One circumstance connected with that funeral ought to be mentioned. Some years before, when the good Catholic Bishop Cheverus died, and funeral services were held in the "Church of the Holy Cross," the bell on the Federal Street Church was tolled by Dr. Channing's particular request, as a token of respect for his memory. The Catholics did not forget it; and now the bell on the "Church of the Holy Cross" in Franklin Street pealed forth a requiem in honor of an uncanonized but truly catholic saint.

In conclusion, dear friends, — for I have spoken too long — I will say, Let us, in honoring a prophet of the past, not forget to honor and love the prophets of our own time, — the true messengers of God, who live and move among us! [Applause.]

The CHAIRMAN. — We would ask the audience to rise and sing, to the tune of "America," the first and the last two stanzas, on the printed slip, of the Memorial Hymn for the Centennial Anniversary, written for this occasion by the venerable Dr. William Newell, of Cambridge, Mass., who had some personal acquaintance with Dr. Channing, and who has also sent us a letter, which will be published with others that have been received, but which cannot all be read now for lack of time.

MEMORIAL HYMN.

By REV. WM. NEWELL, D.D.

And now abideth Faith, Hope, Charity.— I. COR. xiii., 13.
Charity rejoiceth in the Truth.— I. COR. xiii., 6.
And the Truth shall make you free.— JOHN viii., 32.

All hail, God's angel, Truth!
In whose immortal youth
  Fresh graces shine:
To her sweet majesty,
Lord, help us bend the knee,
And all her beauty see,
  And wealth divine.

Thanks for the might of Faith,
That fears not change or death
   Under God's care;
Bringing the distant nigh
To the soul's quickened eye,
And soaring to the sky
   On wings of prayer.

Thanks for the light of Hope,
As through the mist we grope
   Toward heaven's far goal;
On each dark cloud it shines,
Illuming God's designs
Where ill with good combines
   To round the whole.

Thanks for the heart of Love,
Kin to our Lord's above,
   Tender and brave;
Ready to bear the cross,
To suffer pain and loss
And earthly good count dross,
   In toils to save.

Thanks for the names that light
The path of Truth and Right,
   And Freedom's way;
For him whose life doth prove
The might of Faith, Hope, Love,
Thousands of hearts to move,
   A power to-day!

May his dear memory be
True guide, O Lord, to thee,
   With saints of yore;
And may the work he wrought,
The truth of God he taught,
The good for man he sought,
   Spread evermore.

The CHAIRMAN.— We are very glad to see present with us Dr. Hall, Rector of the Church of the Holy Trinity in this city. We all know his large and liberal spirit, and need not to be assured beforehand of his interest in such an occasion as this. I know he will respond to our call upon him, and that you will all rejoice to hear him.

REMARKS OF CHARLES H. HALL, D.D.

It is a long time since I have felt so great an anxiety as I do now to speak, or so profound a conviction that to do so would be an impropriety. You must be talked out by this time. I should be very glad if I had time to follow out one idea, which of course it would be simply impossible to follow out at this time; namely, the place of Channing in the history of our various faiths as they are related to us to-day. I must, then, only touch the salient points.

We drop from a man's name after he is dead, if he has been good for anything, his ordinary Christian titles and the honorary degrees that he may have picked up and carried as a burden along the path of life; and therefore I speak of him whose memory we celebrate to-day simply by his one name, *Channing*.

It is claimed that Channing was a Unitarian; but, in the graveyard where he sleeps, denominational lines are wholly lost sight of. Although, according to the vicious habit which prevails in Greenwood, and I presume in Mount Auburn, they may put chains about the lots, and build up stone-walls around them, and erect hideous structures that make the place unsightly, and take away all natural beauty from it, yet under ground there are no distinctions. And in the blessed shrines of the Church of Souls above it there are none. There, I presume, "all hearts confess the saints elect." The value of Channing to every one of us, whether he was a Unitarian or a Baptist or a Presbyterian or a Methodist or an Episcopalian, or what not, is simply very precious. He did manfully the work which was given him to do.

When the Puritans came to this country in 1620, it was a tremendous change for John, the Puritan. Being persecuted, he came over here to be a persecutor. He did not persecute more than others, but he did something in that bad way. I hide under the name of Prescott, who says that he came hither to establish religious liberty for *himself*,— not, as it proved, for all other men as well. He came over here to assume a totally new relation. He came over here with the tremendous gift of Calvinism, and it is an awful gift for any man to bear!

I reverence old John Calvin, while I differ with him, though perhaps not so much in his ultimate thought. That ultimate thought in his system, as I look at it, was, with such doctrinal materials as he found ready to his hands, to assert the superiority of an illuminated personal conscience against the tyranny of an objective sacerdotal church. I do not know that I differ with anybody in the ultimate thought. I reverence him as I do great names in my own Church, whom I estimate, not so much by what they did as by the spirit which was in their hearts.

Well, the Puritans had had persecutions to keep them together in England, and they came over here to be governors, constructors, and builders. They had a tremendous work.

Singularly enough, the first difficulty which they encountered was in regard to the sacrament. The first great pressure that bore upon them was the sacramental question, though it did not take precisely that definite form.

John, the deacon's son, when he came to be of age, was to be a voter; and Sally, the daughter of the other deacon across the way, was to be married to John. And the question came up as to what should be their relations — civil and ecclesiastical — to the village and to the Church. John said, "I love the meeting, I love the deacons, I love the whole thing, and I believe all you say; but I have not been struck by lightning, I have not had that which every one of the members say they have had."

Under oppression, they had been driven in upon the

centre, and they remained as one body; but the attempt to settle the questions how Sally's children should be baptized, and how John should be allowed to be a voter and a civil officer, agitated New England up to the time when old Dr. Samuel Stoddard, of Northampton, having at last lost faith in the old device of "the half-way covenant," struck out a most peculiar sacramental idea, which our ritualistic friends in my section of the Church are to-day striving to fructify upon; namely, that, though no man could put himself where the lightning is going to strike, yet by the sacraments he could get where he ought to be in case the lightning did strike. Dr. Stoddard, in his "Appeal to the Learned," in 1705, wrote an admirable tract, a copy of which you will find in the Yale College Library. He adopted a system of reasoning on the sacrament to the effect that, while the sacrament would not give an individual the conviction of his personal election, it was a means to that grace; and that, therefore, John and Sally, and all such, should take it, if they would promise to put themselves where the elective decree ordinarily came to an issue.

That device became the acknowledged system of church membership of Northampton, when Jonathan Edwards, that magnificently terrible man, whom none of us can honor or differ from too much, came to be the assistant minister of his maternal grandfather, Dr. Stoddard.

Now we are all Unitarians, Presbyterians, and good fellows together here to-day; and we all have in our hearts, I suppose, about what that grand man, the young Edwards,— and I honor and love his memory almost as much as if I had known him,— felt, when finding, as I think he was correct in concluding he found, that that system must go down unless it could be saved from its own works, he struck out the idea that, at whatever cost, every man must stand on his sense of divine manhood, illuminated by the thought of the election of God, with no compromise or "half-way covenant." With the most rigid Calvinism,— more rigid than the platforms of Cambridge and Boston and Saybrook, and more rigid even than the Westminster Catechism,— he attempted to carry out that "revival" system, as it is now called, which shook New England to the centre. Just then came in that blundering Irishman, ordained of Providence to bring the hidden thoughts of men to light by his surpassing eloquence and his intolerable egotisms, Whitefield, "whose shade through history halts," as Whittier well says. The issue of his New England career was the remorseless test put to every man of the sternest Calvinism or its most decided negative. Compromise was at an end. It was Calvinism, pure and simple, or a new departure. Then followed the two Tennents, Scotch-Irish Presbyterians, of New Jersey. Then came the fanatical Davenport, of Southold, Long Island. And so came about what is called by Congregational historians "the Great Awakening" of 1740.

From that time, it was predestined that there should be two opposite movements, a Channing movement on the one side, and a "revival" movement with Nettleton and other thorough Calvinists on the other side; and it seems to me that this man that we are speaking of to-day must, to his own friends, as they stood nearer and nearer to him, have appeared almost with an aureole upon his head, evidently sainted before he was taken away. It is the simplest thing in the world for us to stand here and recognize the true pedestal on which he stood in the history of that movement which was born in 1740. He did not create it, for it began long before he was influenced by it. It was the effort of the New England conscience to escape from the awful dogmas of Edwards,— to find its way back to what I conceive to be a better gospel. The real object was to save the gospel and reject the iron system which called itself by that holy name. Therefore, it was long known as Arminianism, then, after Channing had passed through the paths of Arianism, as Socinianism, or Unitarianism.

As a boy, Channing must have had extraordinary keenness of perception and tenderness of conscience. It was the death of his father, I think, that went down into his soul and stirred it to its depths, and brought him to a conscious religious life, and to a constant thought of it ever afterwards; and then, almost the first man that came in contact with him, and made an impression upon his religious life,—as some old dominie has first made his profound impression upon us when we were boys,—and guided his mind, and turned his thought, was Dr. Samuel Hopkins.

Dr. Hopkins was a pupil of Jonathan Edwards; and I think I am correct in saying that, as such, he had accepted almost entirely Edwards' theological system. He accepted with it another idea, which many of the best of the pagans have held, which, if treated as unskilful men often do, you may make seem fearful; or you may use it wisely, and may make it shine with the very brightness of God's presence. That idea was, roughly, that a man should so live that he shall feel more or less willing to be damned, if it be God's will, for His glory. It is an old Stoical notion, which has run through the human race from its beginning. And it affected Hopkins powerfully; and I imagine that it begat William Ellery Channing. The first of the books that he was profoundly interested in in college was Hutchinson's "Ideas of Beauty and Virtue," which drilled him in that same general idea, that, benevolence could not have a selfish origin. Take that principle, and follow it through his earlier writings, and you find the man filled with its natural results. And, by the way, let me say that we have all been a little incorrect here this morning in supposing or talking as if Channing had been brought up a Unitarian. The thing, as it appears to us to-day as a rounded system, is not the thing as it appeared to men in 1780. It was then the division or balance between the two sections of the orthodox order,— the Congregational system itself.

I remember that my dear old friend, "Rabbi" Stuart, of Andover, always spoke of the Unitarians as *Arminians;* that is, as the antagonists of Calvin. So I say to you Unitarians here to-day that I am a better Unitarian than you are; because, with all your admiration for Channing, I do not see that you recognize when he gave up his Arianism. And I say — I say it frankly anywhere — that I worship ONE God with all my soul; and I say, looking at the Redeemer of men, that I will not allow any being or creature, however supernal, to stand between the man Christ Jesus and the One infinite God. He was *God manifest in the flesh;* and to me he is not merely a sort of being superior to archangels.

It seems to me perfectly clear that that was the system which Channing received as a boy, and which entered into all his life. He antagonized Calvinism, as it had appeared in the Congregational life of New England. He believed profoundly that benevolence could not have a selfish origin; and he was willing to accept any opprobrium or persecution for the faith that God is all good, and could wish no evil thing. I love to trace the roots of his life-thoughts back into the age before him. For, talk as you please about it, that glorious New England thought, that grand old Calvinistic life, certainly begat men and women. They brought that life up to that point where reaction in dogma was inevitable, their mistakes bringing them here to rigid Calvinism, and bringing them there to freer thought. And at last the Master had occasion for another mode of education. And God, in his mysterious providence, gave to this delicate, sickly boy his wonderful power simply to *love truth for asserting itself,* simply to throw himself in the way of everything that was good and beautiful and kindly and tender, and to utter always the right word and the right thought to his troubled age. As I read his writings, I confess that the chief point about the man is, to my thought, that he was like crystal. I always see through him. I do not stop to think that he was a Yankee, and that I was born in Georgia; or that he sympathized with the abolitionists, while I was taught to detest them. I forget that he was a Unitarian, and that he had ideas about war that I cannot agree with. I care nothing for those things that are merely upon the surface. I recognize that there was in him — always, and in all that he did, and I honor any man in whom it is found — this one thought, "What evil is in me I dare not throne above." In that creed of Channing, on that platform of all true souls, I shake hands with you to-day. [Applause.]

The CHAIRMAN.— We are glad to find Dr. Hall so good a Unitarian, and we cordially extend to him the right hand of fellowship. I see Mr. Mayo here, from Springfield. He has, as you are aware, devoted much time to the subject of education; and who, better than he, can speak to us of Channing's gospel of education for the people? He will now address you.

REMARKS OF REV. A. D. MAYO.

Mr. Mayo, coming forward, read the following paper on the subject assigned to him : —

Ladies and Gentlemen, — Like all reformers of the first class, Channing was possessed by one radical idea; and he blazed that into the souls of a generation for a quarter of a century. That principle was the native dignity of man, and his ability, spite of his misfortunes, frailties, and sins, of responding to great appeals and efforts for his growth toward God and the sublime gospel of Christ the Lord. He flung the central light of this mighty illuminating fact off into the darkness of the three great realms of public life in our New World. He shot a broad, radiant vista down the gloomy tangle the Church, the State, and the school were already becoming, even in the chief republic of the New World.

Only ten years ago, the great Italian statesman, Count Cavour, on his death-bed, whispered to his priest, "*But, father, remember, a free Church in a free State.*" He knew that a Constitutional Monarchy in Europe could only stand on these two pillars,— a free Church in a free State. In a remarkable letter, written in the midst of the Italian Revolution, he said, "A Republic is impossible in Europe, except as the result of the thorough education of the people; and that is the work of the coming century."

Things go faster this side the water; and, more than fifty years ago, William Ellery Channing saw, as clearly as Count Cavour in our day, that the American Republic could never be built up on a paper Constitution and fond recollections of the fathers. As Abraham Lincoln was always saying: "The country can only be saved by the people of the country. No man is great enough to save this Union." Channing saw, before many of us were born, that there were three great reactionary currents running athwart republican institutions in American life. First, there was the old superstition in the Church, which had come down from Europe, not improved, but rather vulgarized in the transit. Second, there was the false political status of the government, ruled as it was in the interests of an arrogant institution, the worst relic of ancient barbarism. Third, there was the gross ignorance of great masses of the people; no State at that time, outside New England, having a system of popular education worthy the name. Only by looking at what Channing did, in view of this alarming state of American affairs sixty years ago, can we make a fair estimate of the man. His work was more thorough, far-seeing, logical, and statesmanlike than had been attempted by any man before that day.

We leave it to others more worthy to tell how he flashed the calcium light of that mighty gospel of the native dignity and improvability of man right into the twilight maze of the American Church and the American State, as they existed two generations ago. But it has been a great satisfaction to us, within the past few months, when our attention has been especially turned to the impending question of the improved education of the whole American people, to see with what clearness, profoundness, and breadth he comprehended this theme. We are somewhat acquainted with the literature of popular education in the English-speaking countries, and we affirm that no writer has left that vast and complex subject so completely in the light as this man. After two generations of improved school-keeping in Great Britain and America, even after the timely reinforcement of valuable methods and theories of various degrees of merit from the continent, the student of pedagogics will find in a few hundred pages in the writings of Channing the most wonderful prophecy and thorough comprehension of all that is most durable and vital in what we call "The New Education."

The essays in which Dr. Channing treated this theme are: his admirable lecture on "Self-culture," which should be printed and dropped into the pocket of every American youth; his remarkable discourses on "The Elevation of the Laboring Classes," "Education," "National Literature," "The Present Age," "The Duty of Children"; and a striking series of letters, petitions, and memoranda, occupying some forty pages in the third volume of his Memoirs. But all his published works and correspondence gleam with side-lights thrown upon this topic, which, as the interesting

Memoir of Elizabeth Peabody shows, occupied so much of his deepest thoughts. What a noble monument to his memory could be reared by a memorial volume of his sayings on the education of the people! Can the religious denomination that has given to America a Horace Mann, a William Eliot, an Edward Everett, a Samuel J. May, a Hosmer, a Thomas Hill, and scores of coworkers, do a better work to-day than gather these papers into such a volume, or, better yet, flood the land with them, printed as separate tracts?

It is not easy, even for our Far-Western friends who may be present to-day, to realize the state of education in America eighty-six years ago, when young William Ellery Channing, at the age of fifteen, became a student in Harvard College. He has left us a quaint picture of the University life of that day, with Cambridge, Boston, Richmond, and Newport, the four points around which his school-life for eight years revolved. We all know what it was. The few colleges in the country were a feeble reflection of the great schools of England in their organization and methods of instructions. One advantage they had. Already, at that early day, the American college invited every ambitious boy to climb "the ladder from the gutter to the University," of which the English Huxley speaks. But, after these and a few dozen academies of secondary instruction and the meagre common schools of the leading New England States, the country was almost an educational waste. Indeed, up to the year 1837, when Horace Mann was appointed first secretary of the Massachusetts Board of Education, although there had been a steady improvement of the American sectarian college and academy, the idea of the free, unsectarian education of the whole people, as now realized in the noble school systems of our North-western States,—a system that leads the child from the little district school through the University, founded upon the magnificent bequest of public lands by the National Government, and supplemented by State, local, and often private aid,— had not been comprehended by the American people.

This is the American system of popular education. It will remain the American in distinction from all other national systems, because it grew out of the primary wants of the American people at the most critical and formative period of its history. The details of the system will be rearranged by every generation, are being modified by every locality to-day. But the system will remain,— at peace with other systems, if they will have peace. But, if they declare war and go before the people, they must expect the lesson that every party and every interest is sure to receive, that plants itself across the track of an American institution. We read that, on the first day the railway train flew across the great Western plateau, a huge bison, in view of his admiring herd, charged down with crushing force upon the oncoming monster. The only record of that conflict was written on the cow-catcher of the lightning express. The final memorials of the campaign of our Cardinal and all corporations, secular or sacred, that lead the assault upon the American free school, will be a few stains and fragments, caught or flung off in the decisive moment of that victorious day.

In laying the foundations of our free education in the common schools of New England and the national benefaction of public domain to the North-west, some of the fathers knew just what they were about. They understood that education does not mean the moulding of childhood and youth into a docile subject of infallible spiritual or secular authority under the hand of a despotic pedagogue or priest. They felt in their bones that the education of the American people must be taken out of the hands of the University scholars, the literati, and the priesthood. Not one of these classes, as a class, even to this day, has shown a worthy apprehension of this mighty enterprise. They placed the public schools of all grades under the sole direction of the people. Not that the majority of the people are school-men, or very intelligent in educational affairs. But the people alone can be trusted to keep the schools out of the hands of the exclusive classes that in the Old World have shut out the masses from the feast of knowledge since the dawn of history. If that advantage could be secured, it was felt that the Republic could wait a century for the best organization and method in public schools, and that as the result of numerous experiments in a region so vast and a population so varied, aided by the whole experience of past and present abroad, the best way might be found of educating the whole people for citizenship in this growing Republic. Nothing so wise, so far-reaching as an act of Christian statesmanship, was ever done in this world as the establishment, without civic parade or clash of arms, of the present free school system of the United States. By the side of it, all British, Romish, or German systems are dwarfed, like the temporary bridges thrown up by our engineers in the late war for getting at or getting out of the way of the enemy beside the majestic span that links the divisions of the Metropolis of the New World.

The reason that this system will endure is that it is founded on the same rock that is the corner-stone of a free Church and a free State. That stone, which so many nation-builders rejected, the very head of our corner, is the faith in the native worth of man and his capacity for indefinite growth under the lead of divine Providence, amid the thronging opportunities of the coming age. Channing always declared that the one reason why we should educate the child of the laboring man is not that we may have a more skilful workman, a better subject of the State, or a more obedient disciple of the Church; but because he is a child of Almighty God, a brother of all men, an heir of immortality, called to be a sovereign in a republican society. It is beautiful to see the steady growth of this great, open-minded, progressive statesman of the closet on this theme. He began with some of the conventional notions of the old New England aristocracy of scholars and ministers,— that the child of the laboring man should only be reared up to the limit of what his superiors might call "his station in life." In an article in the *Reformer*, at an early date, he argues against the general proposition to give the children of the poor the extreme advantages of the rich, at public expense. He appears also to have been taken, as a good many people are to-day, with the impracticable notion of manual labor-schools. But he never returned to that line of reasoning. Indeed, his words to-day read like a quiet sarcasm upon the sort of education then given to the wealthy classes in the higher schools and colleges of America. At one time, he seems to have been interested in an endeavor to utilize Harvard College for the secondary English education of young men of business, something like the " preparatory department " now existing in many of our collegiate schools. He addressed a letter to Josiah Quincy, the President of Harvard, urging this view.

But none of these side-issues long detained this great, clear-eyed apostle of humanity. He learned very early that no sect in religion and no caste in society or scholarship will ever propose, of itself, to do more than educate the people up to what it regards the fit sphere of the masses, in a system of which itself is the head. So he gave his hand, with himself behind it, to Horace Mann, on his acceptance of the modest office of secretary of the new Board of Education for the State of Massachusetts,— an office without a clerkship, with a salary of fifteen hundred dollars, and all Massachusetts, out of doors, for an unexplored field of operation. In a letter written from Newport, Aug. 19, 1837, — a letter that must have blown the fiery soul of Horace Mann to a flame of consecrated zeal, — he wrote: "You could not find a nobler station. Government has no nobler one to give. You must allow me to labor under you, according to my opportunities. If we can but turn the wonderful energy of this people into a right channel, what a new heaven and earth must be realized among us!" And, later, in an admirable speech at a common school convention at Taunton, Mass., he "blessed God that Horace Mann had undertaken this great cause. He cheered him on, and it was ever his prayer that Heaven would give him success."

This interest was not alone the vague and uninstructed interest in educational reform which public men in the North have always been ready enough to express.

It was a most radical, careful, and practical apprehension of just what this reform proposed to do, and what was sure to be its out-come. He felt in his soul the wretched apology for education that was then doled out to the people of New England in the district school of half a century ago. About all there was of it were the few superior teachers, men and women, who got into it; the atmosphere of freedom surrounding it; and the vital interest of a portion of the clergy and people in its support. He hit the nail on the head and drove it home, when he said, "The teacher is the school." He rejoiced at the establishment of the first Normal School in Massachusetts, and proposed what, after half a century, the President of Harvard College has just suggested and some of the State Universities of the West adopted, — a chair of pedagogics in all colleges. This year the venerable Barnas Sears, the Nestor of American education, who links the old New England of Horace Mann with the new Virginia of Dr. Ruffner, in response to the same idea, will mass his appropriation from the Peabody Fund for a great summer institute of country school-teachers at the State University in Charlottesburg.

He anticipated our improved methods of instruction, which are to a school what our labor-saving machinery and the new applications of science are to our modern life. Through Dr. Follen, he had become acquainted with Pestalozzi and the great German authors on didactics; and such men as Channing are apt to read the best book on all vital subjects. And certainly no modern disciple of these great masters more clearly apprehends the reasons for this method of teaching which aims, first, to awaken the love of knowledge; then to develop all powers in their order, using the physical world and the contact with a real teacher as the best library for the infant mind. He insisted that the soul of the child must be led directly to the outward world, taught to open its eyes and use its faculties in the natural way, then led inward to the contemplation of the spiritual world, and all the time kept in vital relations with common life. After beating out its brains for thousands of years in the attempt to run down nature, Education now, beginning in the people's primary school, is following the lead of nature and Providence, teaching and training the child as a good mother educates her little one, and the Divine School-master develops the manhood and womanhood of every obedient son and daughter of God. He understood that such a mighty reform could alone come up from the people, and trusted it would in time reach up to the most exclusive seats of learning. In this, he was a true prophet; for his large idea of a University is now being realized, and the time has come when the sons of the wealthy and famous can really hope to obtain, in Harvard, Yale, and Columbia, a training as natural and fruitful in its methods as thousands of little Irish Patricks, German Minas, and young American citizens of African descent are getting to-day in the primary school-rooms of Cambridge, New Haven, and New York.

In his outlook for the education of the people, Dr. Channing was as unlimited as in his teaching concerning freedom in Church or State. He scorns the idea of setting bounds to the training even of the humblest poor. He declares that, in view of a work so vast and far-reaching as the schooling of an American child, all considerations of wealth, rank, and caste dwindle to insignificance. He gave short shrift to that chimera of "over-education" which is the "spook" of some of our anxious leaders of society. False education of many sorts there can be, and is, nowhere more than in universities and professional schools, with venerable names; but "over-education" he believed impossible. No human being can be too deeply conscious of his own divine nature, obligation, and destiny; can too completely develop all his powers; can hunger and thirst too much for wisdom; can become too intelligent in every station of life. Indeed, on this point, he always insisted that the laboring man, the man of affairs, the mother in the home, needed especially the expanding and uplifting influence of education to open their eyes to the sacredness of common life, to work by intelligent methods, and relieve labor in America from the drudgery it has always been in the nations of the Old World. And what a commentary on his gospel of enlightened industry is our country to-day, where ninety per cent. of our men of business fail, and every city resounds with the conflict between capital and labor, and two million children on Southern soil are unschooled, and Massachusetts contains one hundred thousand people unable to read and write! The man who studied himself to a skeleton in the little out-house where he lived as the tutor of a proud Richmond family knew well enough that, if you make education what it should be, there is no danger that any child will go to school to shirk work or fool away its years in a long holiday. Make the schools of America the best, and place real teachers in them, and only the children who are competent to mount the rugged way that the best mental discipline always must be will reach the higher grades of school-life. Meanwhile, the great masses will be better fitted for the mighty responsibilities of citizenship in the Republic at fifteen than the graduate of Oxford or Berlin to be a sovereign voter in a union of sovereign people.

One word more. Whoever reads Channing carefully will see that never, for a moment, was he bitten with that plausible fallacy of ultra "Secularism" in popular education which is having its run in some quarters, even among the Protestant clergy. Of course there is a certain plausibility in the wholesale declaration of the Pope: Either religious education, according to the mandate of the infallible Head of the Church, or an education from which all acknowledgment of God and spiritual existence, and even morality as dependent on religion, shall be expurgated. Channing saw most clearly that the real difficulty in this matter in America is with the clergy, and very little with the people. Every body of the clergy, from Catholic to Quaker, as a class, is tempted to indorse the position of the Pope: Either teach religion in public schools as we understand it, or sweep the school-room floor clean of everything but mental training and morality cut loose from every sanction of religious faith. But, happily, the American system of government and the public school, which is the soul of our government, were established, not by a treaty between clergy and laity, but by direct action of the whole people. And the American people, at the beginning, made a new departure concerning religion in public affairs, even more important to civilization than the Protestant Reformation in Europe.

That departure assumes the existence through all Christendom of what Dean Stanley so happily calls "a common Christianity." That common Christianity consists of the few beliefs and faiths that are common to the great mass of good citizens of every church and every condition, in all Christian lands,—the profound faith in the obligation of all men to worship Almighty God, obey Christ's law of love, and live in view of the immortal life, which is the rock-bed of religion as taught in the New Testament. It is that common Christianity which separates Christendom from the rest of the world; which underlies the society, the culture, the legislation, the language, the whole form and substance of life in Christian lands, and creates the spiritual atmosphere into which every child in Christendom is born. The American people is the first in history that has comprehended that fact at the beginning, and held to it "without variableness or shadow of turning." The American common school, like the American government, society, life in every particular, assumes the transcendent obligation of this common Christianity and the public and private morality which is its practical side.

Our public school knows nothing of Catholic or Protestant, Jew or Infidel, Pagan or Christian, in the technical sense in which those words are fought over in the schools of theology. But the common school, from the first, has lived and breathed in the vital atmosphere of that common Christianity which is the real conviction of all but the eccentric few. For, however faulty may be the private or public morality of Americans, American public opinion insists that children shall be trained according to the common Christianity, which is the unwritten moral constitution of the Republic. The chief religious trouble in common schools has been the attempt of the more zealous clergy of different churches to force into them their own sectarianism. The mass of the people will no longer submit to that. But when any branch of the clergy or any class of politicians strikes hands with public Atheism, and says, "This Republic has no God, and human government has no foundation but the shifting opinions of men, and the American school is utterly secular," the American people, which has always been a century ahead of any American professional class in its comprehension of public religion and morality, says: "Not so. Our school remains, like our government, living and breathing in the atmosphere of the common Christianity. To ask us to take it out of this common moral atmosphere of Christendom, and try to work it in the rarefied ether of your philosophical secularism, is like proposing that a full-grown man shall step into an exhausted receiver to cast his vote for president. Grown men, of common sense, cannot live in either a physical or spiritual vacuum; and the American people will keep the American common school on the *terra firma* of the common Christianity, spite of the subtleties of the secularist or the threats of our Cardinal.

Dr. Channing was born with the Republic, and grew up as a public man, the very incarnation of the American idea of public life. With his whole soul, he abhorred the clerical intolerance that worried the fathers from the beginning, and defended the right, even of Abner Kneeland, to have his private say on religion. But no man more clearly saw the absurdity and the impossibility of working a nation on the assumption that there is no God, no eternal code of morality, no spiritual and immortal life. Every word he wrote concerning the education of the people is radiant with reverence for man as the child of God, living in a providential order of human affairs. No man more completely than he represents the practically unanimous resolve of our people — never more pronounced than to-day — that character training and public morality shall be a paramount element in the American common school, and the basis of that training in private and public virtue shall be the common Christianity which is the soul of all progress in Christian lands.

We have spoken of Channing's gospel of education for the people. It was indeed a gospel. Nowhere so clearly, in such luminous lines, as in his pages, will the friend of education find this underlying and all-including inspiration of the American free school. There may the anxious parent, the weary teacher, the vexed school-man, the discouraged statesman go, as to a bath in the fountain of perpetual youth, and renew a drooping faith by communion with the deep heart of the little child. The children of America to-day should rise up and bless that glorious, childlike man who all his life pleaded and toiled for them in the face of an unbelieving world. In the good day of the children, which is dawning upon us, the name William Ellery Channing will shine with a mild, perpetual light, like a fixed star beaming out of the highest heaven. [Applause.]

The CHAIRMAN.— We must hear from some of our Universalist friends. Rev. Mr. Nye, pastor of the "Church of Our Father" in this city, is with us here to-day. We regret to learn that he is about to leave Brooklyn for another field of labor. Before he goes, however, he must leave with us his thought about Channing.

REMARKS OF REV. H. R. NYE.

I believe I would have preferred, at this hour, to have kept my seat. I have a bit of an address somewhere in my pocket, but I shall utter only two or three words to you now.

The sympathy existing between the Universalist and the Unitarian churches now is, of course, much greater than that of former times. Dr. Putnam, the pastor of this church,

—and that accounts probably for so many excellent things in his character, his spirit, and life,— was brought up in the Universalist Church, and, if I am not incorrect, in a Universalist family. I was brought up in a Congregationalist family, and my father was a Congregationalist clergyman; and I can remember very well the early times in my boyhood days, before the rupture had taken place between the Trinitarian Congregationalists and the Unitarian Congregationalists,— the time to which the Rector of the Holy Trinity Church referred,— when the Unitarians were Arminians, and when the name "Unitarian" was scarcely known; and you remember that it was scarcely known at all until after the war with England in 1812. I can remember very well that then my father, though a Congregational clergyman, was accustomed to exchange with the Rev. Dr. Crosby, the Unitarian pastor, twelve miles distant. The rupture was not quite complete in that direction. Now we are very near together. You may remember Starr King said—and he said many brilliant things concerning the Universalists and the Unitarians—that the Universalists believed that God was too good to damn any human being absolutely forever, and that the Unitarians believed that human beings were too good to be damned.

I honor Dr. Channing for his loyalty to Christ and his broad Christian charity. He believed firmly in different interpretations of the Christian faith. There is the Methodist interpretation; there is the Baptist interpretation; there is the Congregationalist interpretation; and there is the Episcopalian interpretation; and, if you please, they are all Christian, and they stand at last upon the one Foundation and honor the one Name. Jesus Christ is above them all, he being the Master, and we only the learners and pupils in his school. That is the reason why we, in one sense, so largely revere Dr. Channing.

I have a wife, at home, who was in Dr. Channing's Sunday-school. I hold in my hand a sermon preached by Dr. Channing in the year 1819, the year that I was born. I remember that Dr. Channing died in 1842, the year that I was ordained. Somehow, I put these thoughts along in this manner together. In the year 1842, it was my utmost desire to hear this great man preach; but I could not, and it was never my privilege to put my eyes upon his face. But for two things the name of Channing is to me exceedingly precious: first, for his love of truth, wherever to be found; and next for his love of man. And I ask you to remember to-day that in no ancient religion of which any man can speak, and in no ancient philosophy, was there ever such an idea of man as Christianity presents to us; and that, in Christianity, in its grand idea of every man a child of God and every man a spiritual and birthright heir of the immortal life, lies all that is sweetest and tenderest and noblest in the teaching of Channing. I honor him for his love of truth and for his love of man; and I am very glad to utter these few words, which I do with the profoundest reverence, in my whole heart, for the beautiful spirit of his life, for the power which his example has exerted upon the age since he passed away, and for the good which his books have done to my own soul in the Christian life. [Applause.]

Dr. Gottheil of the Temple Emmanuel, New York, being seen in the audience, Rev. Mr. Camp was requested to invite him to come forward and offer his testimony. As he stepped upon the platform, he was greeted with hearty applause.

REMARKS OF REV. DR. GUSTAV GOTTHEIL.

Is there room in this place,— I ask not for much, as I do not intend to detain you for any length of time,— is there room in this place for the hand of a Jew to lay a flower on the honored grave of this apostle of love and freedom? [Applause.] Is there room for one of the ancient people to express his admiration for, and his great obligation to, the man whose birthday you celebrate? In accepting the invitation that was kindly extended to me to join in this celebration, I hoped to be among the silent participants; but, just as Mr. Chadwick confessed himself to lie helplessly under the spell of the honored pastor of this church, so I avow myself to be in the power of one of his brethren, Mr. Camp. We Jews have recently been celebrating the anniversary of our fathers' emancipation from Egyptian bondage. I did not feel at that time that there was any one chain about me which I should never be able to break; but Brother Camp undeceived me when, a few moments ago, he came to me with the command that I had to say something. I begged for mercy, but he was implacable. He would give me no release. So you must forbear with me, and pardon the crude state of my remarks, as I had not even the privilege of Brother Chadwick in regard to time for preparation. I take, however, courage from the consideration that, where the heart is full, the least preparation often proves the best.

As many of those who have preceded me referred to some personal recollections, permit me to do so in my turn.

Some twenty years ago, I made my entry into an English-speaking community, at Manchester, England, profoundly ignorant of the mysteries of the English tongue. The president of my congregation came to me one morning, when I was just setting out on the dangerous journey to discover the island where the treasures of English thought and feeling are to be found, and, handing me two volumes, said: "Here, this is an American classic. Study him." I opened the books. They were the works of William Ellery Channing. So you see that my acquaintance with your apostle is contemporaneous with one of the most important changes in my life.

Since that time, I have never ceased to read these works over; and it would be hard for me to convey to you, even if I had had time to prepare, the feelings with which I, a descendant of that ancient race which has fought so long and paid so dearly for the great truth of the unity of God and the brotherhood of man, listened to the solemn accents that fell from the lips of this immortal man; when I heard him solemnize and glorify this central and vital doctrine in accents which I had never heard before, and, to be frank with you, which I never have heard again, from any one professing Christianity.

I came still nearer him through the medium of one in whose friendship I rejoice, and who has always appeared to me to stand to him in the relation in which John the Evangelist is said to have stood to his Master. I refer to Dr. Bellows. He gave me a new and deeper interest in the works of the great divine; and I think I shall not dishonor his memory if I take his name, next Sabbath day, to my own pulpit, and pay him the tribute which is due to one who stood forth the devoted and eloquent champion of liberty and the emancipation of the slave, the apostle of human dignity and of the immortal greatness of the human soul.

The impression I have gathered from Dr. Channing's writings is that his theory of Christianity cannot be substantiated by the literary or historical proofs on which he relied; but it participated of his own deeply moral nature, his own great mind, his deep and loving heart; he roams, as it were, in the ancient halls, calling to his aid all the spirits which he thought would minister to the ideal which alone could satisfy his own spiritual needs and those of his generation. It is Channing reflected on the historical background which he construed. I look upon the issue which he placed before himself as Channing's ideal, glorious with light and freedom and joy, as against the dark picture of the Church. Though he always meant to speak as a disciple, he, in truth, spoke as a master. You feel, when you read him, that he was much bolder than he knew, and that all his thoughts have the force and freshness of a spontaneous mind, and do not state what he found in the book, but what he discovered in his own reason and conscience.

Since that time, the issue has been transferred to a very different field. The contest now lies between science and religion,— between religion and no religion at all. But, when we trace the way of progress, Dr. Channing will at all times be recognized as one marking a new epoch in the development of Christianity in this country as well as in others. What the issue may be no man can tell; but I believe that the great minds of all ages will ever be held in honor as helpers and coworkers in the advancement of the human mind. I may declare unto you, speaking as to brethren and sisters, gainsaying no man's faith nor insisting upon my own, that I am satisfied to feel the throb of human hearts, as I do now in this temple, in the communion of all the saints, whatever the church that owns them.

I do not ascribe perfection or expect the solution of the last problem to any one church or denomination. Truth would be but a very small thing, hardly worth striving for, if it could be contained within the walls of one church, or if it could be known among men ranging themselves under *one* name only. The human mind is too rich, too abundant in possibilities, for that; and when we leave our narrow bounds, and allow our minds to cross the ocean, and go into distant continents, or recall half-forgotten ages, everywhere we find the same straining of the human mind after the infinite God, though in divers ways and various manner. And, as Goethe says, because men are striving after the highest, they needs must err. No one has yet appeared on this planet in whom all conditions of men could absolutely believe.

Therefore, I join with my whole heart every movement that tends to widen our sphere, to unshackle the soul, and to lift it to the heights where the eternal One, that Being in whom this great man lived and moved, overshadows all others. [Applause.]

The CHAIRMAN. — The time is drawing near when this meeting must be brought to a close. There are many others here whose voices we would fain listen to, and we regret that the needed time is not afforded us; yet, before we sing the concluding hymn, we want to hear a word from Boston. The pastor of the First Church of that city will be one of the speakers to-night at the Academy; but I think that Mr. Foote, minister of King's Chapel, the first of American Unitarian churches, will consent to address you now.

REMARKS OF REV. H. W. FOOTE.

My friends, I did not expect, at this late hour, to say a word to you; and I must say but a very few words.

The beauty of this occasion has been the voice from every other side of Christendom and from beyond it. I suppose that our friend, Dr. Putnam, has called upon me now, that the chord which Channing touched in the city where his work was done might not be wholly wanting here; and certainly I am more than thankful, not to lay a stone on the cairn of a dead prophet, — for, if he were only that, he would be, like many another, almost or quite forgotten, — but to join with you in our triumphant testimony to a life and a work full of vital and vitalizing power.

The single thought that I would like to put into words, in thinking of Dr. Channing, is one that has not been brought out this morning. Perhaps, from being the minister of a very ancient church, I like to trace historic continuity; and so, as I look at Channing's life, it seems to me that sometimes it has been looked at too much as an isolated fact in the spiritual history of America, and that his spiritual pedigree has not been sufficiently recognized. Dr. Hall has told us, most eloquently and vividly and truly, how that is to be traced through the historic line of New England Congregationalism; but there was another factor which, I think, as I ponder Dr. Channing's life, entered more than that into that life, and that was the very blood that beat in his veins.

Channing was a native of the island where, from the beginning, was the colony of religious liberty; and the ideas that throbbed in Roger Williams' heart, in him, blossomed and bore fairer fruit than Roger Williams knew or could foresee. His life as a preacher was passed in Boston, and he did more than Boston can tell to fill it with larger life; yet the most loyal of us Bostonians can see that it was not the spirit most characteristic of Boston that kindled in him, though he strove to make this spirit more. He brought to us ideal elements of character which he did not fully find there, and he made that the place whence his spiritual philosophy and the large light of his generous soul shone as from a beacon set on a hill. His spirit was the spirit of Rhode Island. He was a typical Rhode Islander. That which we have to remember and to rejoice at in him more than any thing that he taught, more than any one of the ideas, great, living, eternal, which were the very heart of his life, is the fact of what he was in himself. His special influence is and must be, chiefly, in the fact that he stands pre-eminently in our modern America for moral ideas. Here was one who lived in these thoughts, whose life was spent in communing with them and in setting them before others, the thoughts the greatest, the ideas the most inspiring, which a soul can touch. Who can estimate the infinite value to his country of a man who is consecrated absolutely to such high, grave themes in this land of hasty speech; in this age of theological indifference, on the one side, or of theological virulence, even now, on the other; in this period so devoured with the lust for material things; in this era of an unspiritual philosophy, when, though the stars shine, there are so many eyes that cannot see their shining? How shall we describe in words glowing enough the value of such a type of character, this mind, so calm, and so patient in waiting for the truth to orb itself in its full light, this soul that lived so absolutely in communion with the great Eternal Thought, — the thought of Christ, of duty, of the human soul, and of the living God? [Applause.]

At the conclusion of Mr. Foote's remarks, the audience rose, and joined in singing the following doxology (Hymn 104 of the Collection) : —

> From all that dwell below the skies,
> Let the Creator's praise arise.

The Chairman then renewed the invitation to all present to repair to the adjoining chapel and basement hall of the church, where committees of ladies were in waiting to receive them to the social festivities of the day.

The benediction was pronounced by Rev. Dr. Peabody, of Cambridge.

SOCIAL FESTIVAL.

At the close of the morning Memorial Meeting at 2 P.M., while large numbers of the friends present returned to their homes or places of sojourn to await the hour of the evening meeting at the Academy, five or six hundred accepted the invitation to the social festival, and soon assembled in the chapel and basement hall of the church. The desk in the chapel had been removed from its platform, which was now thickly set with a variety of flowering plants. Tables bountifully spread with refreshments extended along the centre of the room. A blessing was asked by Rev. George W. Cutter, of Buffalo, N.Y.; and, long after the repast which followed, friends from near and from afar still lingered to talk of the one subject of the day, and to revive memories and traditions of past years.

MEETING IN THE ACADEMY OF MUSIC.

The final meeting of the celebration was held in the Academy of Music on Wednesday evening, April 7, at 7.45 o'clock. Free tickets had been issued for all who wished to attend, and were placed at numerous convenient centres in Brooklyn, N.Y., or sent with circulars of invitation to friends in and out of the city. The Brooklyn *Eagle* of the next day, in its report of the occasion, said: —

"The Academy of Music has rarely, if ever, held such a magnificent audience as that which assembled within its walls last evening to celebrate the one hundredth anniversary of the birth of William Ellery Channing. A large throng waited before the doors were opened to pay homage to the memory of the great preacher and thinker, and eagerly embraced the first opportunity of entering the building. When the portals were unbarred, the multitude, like a mighty torrent released from its bonds, rushed through the doorways and surged over the parquet and along the galleries, submerging every seat in the dense human tide. It was a grand audience that looked up from the main floor and down from the bended bows of the dress and family circles. It embraced a vast representation of thinking Brooklyn, beside delegates from other cities who came to honor Channing and to enjoy the intellectual treat promised in the announcement. All the faces in the throng were reflective of careful attention and profound thought. Fully one-half of the audience was composed of ladies.

The decorations were almost entirely floral. The orchestra stall was turned into a flower-garden. Huge calla lilies, with snow-like bells and darting golden tongues, raised their pure petals from masses of evergreens that screened the facing of the stage. Azaleas, ferns, and potted plants and flowers of numerous varieties filled the entire space between the boxes. Beneath the proscenium arch, in letters of white upon a ground of emerald green, was this reminder, "1780 — Channing — 1880," which had been seen over the pulpit in the church during the morning and afternoon.

Beside the reading-desk bloomed an immense floral cross and star. Its flowers were radiant and fragrant, and showed all their beauties beneath the gleaming gas-jets. An excellent portrait in oil of Channing stood at the head of the centre aisle. The painting was by Ingham, of New York, and is the property of the Rev. Dr. Bellows. It was adorned by an elaborate floral wreath. The perfume of the flowers made fragrant the atmosphere in the auditorium. When the exercises began, every inch of space in the Academy was packed. At least four thousand persons were present."

Beside those who addressed the meeting, there were seated on or near the stage five or six hundred persons, representing the most prominent departments of social, official, literary, and professional life, as well as all sects and parties in the city. Mingled with these were many distinguished ministers and laymen from other places. Included in this general array of citizens and strangers were Mr. Isaac H. Frothingham, President of the Board of Trustees of the Church of the Saviour; Rev. A. P. Peabody, D.D.; Rev. Charles H. Hall, D.D.; Rev. John Cotton Smith, D.D., of the Church of the Ascension, New York; ex-Mayor John W. Hunter; Hon. Dorman B. Eaton, New York; Hon.

Joseph Neilson, Justice of the City Court; Joshua M. Van Cott, Esq.; Hon. J. S. T. Stranahan; Mr. Alexander M. White; Rev. Henry W. Foote, of King's Chapel, Boston; Mr. Josiah O. Low; ex-Judge John Greenwood; Hon. A. W. Tenney; Hon. Ripley Ropes; Capt. Nathaniel Putnam; Prof. R. F. Leighton; Professors A. Crittenden and D. G. Eaton, of the Packer Institute; Rev. J. G. Bass, City Missionary; Mr. R. H. Manning; Rev. J. C. Ager, Pastor of the Swedenborgian Church; Rev. Almon Gunnison and Rev. H. R. Nye, of the Brooklyn Universalist churches; Mr. John T. Howard; Hon. Demas Strong; Col. Rodney C. Ward; Rev. William C. Leonard, of the Church of the Redeemer; Mr. J. G. Hollinshead; Mr. E. W. Crowell; Mr. Gordon L. Ford; Chauncey L. Mitchell, M.D.; Mr. Henry Sanger; Rev. J. W. Chadwick; Mr. Eli Robbins; Mr. Oliver Johnson; Hon. Edwin Reed, Bath, Me.; Messrs. James and Duncan Littlejohn; Rev. Edward Beecher, D.D.; Collector John Tanner; Rev. S. H. Camp; Mr. Reuben W. Ropes; Col. W. B. C. Thornton; Rev. A. D. Mayo, Springfield, Mass.; Dr. Gustav Gottheil, of Temple Immanuel, New York; ex-Mayor Samuel Booth; Mr. George Hannah, Librarian of the Long Island Historical Society; Mr. S. B. Noyes, Librarian of the Brooklyn Library; Prof. G. S. Taylor, of the Adelphi Academy; President David Cochran, of the Polytechnic Institute; Mr. Samuel McLean; Mr. John W. Frothingham; Mr. John W. Wood; Rev. Wayland Hoyt, D.D., of the Strong Place Baptist Church; J. N. Moffat, M.D.; Mr. S. B. Chittenden, Jr.; R. M. Wyckoff, M.D.; Mr. Morris Reynolds; Mr. Alden J. Spooner; Hon. George H. Fisher and Mr. Bernard Peters, of the Brooklyn *Times;* Mr. Horace B. Claflin; Prof. E. T. Fisher; Hon. John Winslow; A. W. Catlin, M.D.; Mr. W. Dodsworth; Hon. John F. Henry; Mr. Lorin Palmer, of the Brooklyn *Union-Argus;* Rev. F. W. Holland, Cambridge, Mass.; Mr.

Andrew McLean, of the Brooklyn *Eagle;* William H. Thayer, M.D.; Hon. J. W. Gilbert, Justice of the Supreme Court; Mr. Joseph R. Blossom; Rev. Henry Powers, Manchester, N.H.; Rev. H. C. Parker, Nashua, N.H.; Rev. Hilary Bygrave, East Milton, Mass.; Gen. John B. Woodward; Mr. W. S. Tisdale; Mr. Stanton Beebe; Rev. Henry Blanchard, Worcester, Mass.; Rev. R. D. Burr, Auburndale, Mass.; Rev. George L. Chaney, Leominster, Mass.; Rev. Frederic Meakin, Taunton; Rev. Charles H. Tindall, Vineland, N.J.; Hon. J. C. Perry; E. N. Chapman, M.D.; and of the members of the Methodist Conference then in session in Brooklyn, Rev. Messrs. Francis, Thompson, Poole, Williams, Buell, Lansing, Brown, Gedney, Taylor, Whedon, Allison, and Seckerson.

Mr. A. A. Low, President of the meeting, and the various speakers for the evening, were greeted with loud applause as they came upon the stage at the appointed hour.

Mr. Low, the President, excused himself from making any opening address, but called on Rev. Dr. Putnam, Chairman of Committee of Arrangements, to offer any introductory remarks that might be necessary. Dr. Putnam said that his speech would simply be the announcement of the first hymn on the printed programme. He would, however, state that all sects and churches in the vicinity, and the public generally, had been cordially invited to join in the commemorative meetings of the day; and he desired, in behalf of the Committee of Arrangements, to thank most heartily the thousands present that they had accepted the invitation in the same spirit in which it had been given. He then requested the assembly to rise, and all join in singing the hymn to the tune, "Hummel."

The audience responded to the call, and were led by a chorus of more than fifty voices from the several Unitarian churches of the city, with organ and cornet accompaniment.

O God! we praise thee, and confess
  That thou the only Lord
And Everlasting Father art,
  By all the earth adored.

To thee all angels cry aloud,
  To thee the powers on high,
Both cherubim and seraphim,
  Continually do cry,—

O holy, holy, holy Lord,
  Whom heavenly hosts obey!
The world is with the glory filled
  Of thy majestic sway.

The apostles' glorious company,
  And prophets crowned with light,
With all the martyrs' noble host,
  Thy constant praise recite.

The holy church throughout the world,
  O Lord! confesses thee,—
That thou eternal Father art,
  Of boundless majesty.

The Rev. George C. Miln, pastor of the East Congregational Church, was then requested to offer prayer.

PRAYER BY REV. GEORGE C. MILN.

O thou Eternal Being in whom we live and move and have our being, our Creator, our Father, our Friend, we rejoice in this opportunity of illustrating our belief in the communion of saints. We rejoice in this opportunity of showing to each other, and to the world, that beneath the superficial conditions of dogmatic statement there is a real unity; that the Christian Church is one, as God is one; that it is one in one Lord, one faith, and one baptism. We rejoice, too, that we have occasion to-day to celebrate the birth of a man who, in his time, did so much to promote that general sympathy between man and man, and between sect and sect, which can but hasten on the coming of the kingdom of God. We rejoice in the record of his life, its sweetness, its loftiness, its purity, its true nobility, and its grandeur. We rejoice in every work, the record of which is left behind, as being performed by him in the interest of our race.

We beseech of thee, O God, to-night, that this assemblage may be prophetic of that day in which thy children shall see eye to eye. We pray that that day in which we shall be lifted out of bondage to any formulated statement of doctrine into the higher spiritual and emotional life may soon dawn upon our waiting eyes. And we pray that wherever men, as he whose life we this day honor did, are seeking to promote between their fellow-men that sympathy and love and sweetness of spirit which is the imitation of Christ's spirit, they may be furthered in that work.

And now, O Lord, we pray that whatever shall be said to-night may tend to unite all those who look toward the Lord Jesus Christ as the pattern for human life and conduct. We pray that it may tend to bind us together in the unity of the spirit and in the bond of peace. Let thy blessing descend upon that great body of Christian people with whom the subject of these services was connected in his life. Grant, O Lord, that their work, great and blessed and prospered as it has been in the past, may go on; and that they may prove, as they have done, their right to a place in the great army of God in the earth.

We beseech of thee to hear us, to be with us, to bless us, and to guide us, in thy name. *Amen.*

The CHAIRMAN.—I am now directed to call upon Rev. Dr. Ellis, of the First Church, in Boston, to address you; and I have the honor to present him to you.

REMARKS OF REV. RUFUS ELLIS, D.D.

Mr. President and dear Friends,—I count it a great privilege to be summoned to this gospel feast. It is always pleasant, it is always helpful, to look up and recall a deservedly famous man. I love to be able to look up, and not to be called upon, as we so continually are in our day, to analyze, to explain, to account for great men; for that is so apt, as you know, to end in explaining them away, and bringing them down to our poor level. We want to look up, and let the light from their faces shine down into ours; and I am sure it is an especial privilege when we can come together, men and women of different minds, of different opinions, — and yet, as we believe, of the same most precious faith, striving to keep the unity of the spirit in the bond of peace, and to be of one heart in one Christian household, if we cannot be just of one mind and of one opinion. It is one of our privileges, as we all see in these days, that we can so come together, and that, when we make up our calendar of saints, we always go beyond our communion, seeking only for those whose love for Christ is true. And because there are so many such seekers, the name that we are naming to-day will be spoken with affection and reverence in many Christian households,— not only Protestant, but Catholic as well; for we know that one of the best eulogiums upon Channing has been pronounced by one of our Roman Catholic brethren.

Now, sir, it does not seem to me hard to find or long to seek, if we wish to know what it is about Channing that so binds us all to him. Why, the very things that have been said about his limitations, the very things that have been said sometimes seemingly in disparagement of him, only help to bring out his characteristic merits more distinctly. They only help to put a frame around the picture. I think we shall all say that he is always, and everywhere, and at all times, and in all his utterances, distinctively a gospel preacher,— one of the great gospel preachers of our age. People object. They say, "Well, he was not a great theologian"; and they are right. His theology was always only popular theology. It was not metaphysical theology. It was not the theology of the schools and of the professors. They add, "He was not distinctively a man of letters"; and I should say, though not quite so confidently, that I think they are right there. I suppose that even his great sermons will hardly go down to posterity among the great English classics. We do not read them now at a sitting. We do not take in every picture eagerly. We do not read to the very last line, just as we sip the last drop of some precious cordial. They are didactic. They are over-diffuse even, I think, for the reader. They are weighty rather than incisive. Even his essays are all sermons. He always preaches. And they say that he founded no sect. He was only incidentally, indirectly, by the way, connected with a sect. They even tell you that he knew very little of the world, — the great world, the world of the statesman, the world of the merchant; that he was a parish minister, and an invalid at that. And that is true, also. But, then, consider, my friends, that, though metaphysical theology has spoiled a great many preachers, it never made one yet, and it is not an essential part of a minister's outfit; and consider, too, — and we Unitarians have had some sad experience in this, — that a man of letters is often wholly lost upon a great congregation of hungry souls, whilst the man who is thought to be unlettered, and never to have been taught anything, will hold an audience sometimes, out on the parish green, that has been lost from the church.

And, then, as to founding a sect, was there ever a great preacher yet who was not a great deal larger than his sect, or who did not come to be, at all events, before he got through? Consider, too, as to knowing men. Why, how many of us know a great many men, know all about what they are saying and doing, and yet know very little about man and what is in man.

Now, we can admit all these things about Channing, only remembering that, when the moral development in a man is very large, it is likely to overshadow the intellect, and we do not think as much of his intellectuality then as we ought. Remember this. And yet, admitting it all, I shall say that Channing was so wondrously endowed with the prophetic function that it amounted, as it always does, to genius, to which you must add learning, as much as you can get of it, and intellect, as much as you can get of it, and poetry, and wit, and rhetoric, and everything else. But, then, all those things are perfectly useless, and always very tedious in the preacher, without the prophetic function. Channing was, first, last, always, a great gospel preacher; and, if you are willing to use the old words in the old sense, you had better say that he was a prophet. Being filled with the spirit of his God, and finding God near him and in him, he prophesied; and the world listened to him. And that is why we are here to-night. And we do not consider, I think, as much as we ought, how preaching has been spoiled by those very things which Channing was said to lack, or how much we have lost and left out of sight that old prophetic speech, — the word which the people in Judea and in Galilee heard so gladly, not irrational truth, not unreasonable truth, but unreasoned truth, truth from the people to the people, truth right out of the abundance of a loving, religious heart. The Word of God, that never returns to a man void, — we are spoiling that continually by what we undertake to add to it. And Channing is to be remembered, not so much for what else he was, — and that was a great deal, — but because he was all else in subordination to this great function of a preacher; and for that, I say, we remember him. In that way, he served his generation; and he is laying his hand upon our hearts to-day, still living and working on.

He came, as such men always do come, in the fulness of the times, — not alone, not unheralded. He came at a time when he was greatly needed, and there was preparation for him. As those of you who heard the sermon of last evening know, it was a time in New England when just such a man was wanted. We had had a dispensation of the letter, which indeed was glorious; but there was needed, as we always need, a fresh dispensation of the Spirit, which should be infinitely more glorious. And it came, and there had been preparation for it. There were tokens of such life in New England before the Revolution. Charles Chauncy, in the old First Church of Boston, was a man of mark, — a man who made, or began to make, an epoch in his time. So was Mayhew, in the West Church. And, before the Revolution, they both of them spoke living words,— not merely words from the old traditions,— and the times went on ripening. There were signs in the New England Congregational body of a reviving of religious life; and it is very narrow, it is a great mistake, to say that it came from only one quarter. It came from both sides of that body,— from those who were called "conservatives," and from those who would have been called, if the word had been used in that day, "liberals." There was a feeling all around that men must come nearer to the reality of Christ's gospel; that they must have something other than what they had been having too much of in New England, and a great deal of in Scotland,— what was called "Moderatism." There were many preachers who had ceased to hold old truths in the old way; and they met the case by saying nothing about them, lest somebody should be hurt, lest the repose of the churches — for it was no better than that — should be disturbed, lest there should be some divisions.

Now, they all began to feel that that was not the way to preach the gospel. And so the more conservative said, "If we are going to have these old doctrines, let us have them, and let us have them clearly and earnestly stated." On the other hand, there was a feeling that the time had gone by for these old statements, and that they must be restated. On both sides, they were reaching out for the reality of the Lord's Word,— the conservatives in their way, and the liberals in their way; and we must not dispose of the whole matter by saying that on the one side it was all bigotry, and that on the other side there were only pale negations. That does not represent the case at all. There were signs of a new life. Channing, in his way, was reaching continually after this great divine reality. He believed that there was still a message in the gospel for men, and he was bound somehow to get it uttered.

He was not alone. You cannot help thinking sometimes, or asking yourself, what might have been the result, if some men who began their career with him had only been permitted to live on. There was a famous man in what was called the Brattle Street Church, one Buckminster (we do not hear his name often in our day),—a man who died at the early age of twenty-eight, and yet left his mark deep in that city,—evidently a man of most earnest spirit, of most wonderful gifts; and another man, one Thatcher, in what was called "The New South Church," who lived a little longer. Both of them were contemporaries of Channing; Buckminster dying in 1812, and Thatcher in 1818, Thatcher only thirty-two or thirty-three years of age at the time of his death, surviving to write the memorial of his friend. These men died in the very bloom of their years. Channing lived on in life-long feebleness, and yet with great power, reaching out after this reality.

We sometimes wish — I am sure I do — that the Congregational body had not been divided, and that Channing might have got at his affirmations in some more direct way, just as the blessed Lord reached his affirmations,— not by discussing with the Jews their theology, but by passing right through the *Halacha* and the *Hagada*, as they called them,— the allegories and the legal niceties that were taught then in the synagogue. He simply passed over them all, paying hardly any attention to them, not destroying, but fulfilling, and went back to the great Book of Deuteronomy and to the prophets, Isaiah and Jeremiah and Ezekiel and Micah, and the rest, building upon them. But such things are not for us men, and Channing must do the best thing he could; and so he became a controversialist, though only for a little while. We wish it could have been otherwise. At least, I do, because the theology of Channing seems to me to be the least interesting part of him. He kept a good deal that he might as well have parted with; and what interests us about him is not this transitional and temporary thing that we call theology, but his Christian consciousness, his faith in Christ as the One who lived in God and for God, and for God's children, and who had a personal message to his soul. That is what he cared for, and compared with that it was of very little consequence in what it happened to be embodied.

It was, in his case, embodied first in Trinitarianism, then in Arianism, and then we can hardly tell in what; but the consciousness remained, and that was the deep living nature in him, and that was what he lived to bring near to men's need; and every day he became less polemical in his preaching. We talk about his theological sermons and his controversial sermons; but they are very few in number compared with the rest of his sermons. He personally got his subjects from the street, and from men's wants and sins, and strove to apply them in the most practical fashion, not as men had been so much in the habit of preaching all around him, seeming to play with their subject, because Sunday had come and there must be a sermon, but as men who had a point to carry, and who believed that Jesus, in his spirit and life, could help them carry it. That was his manner of preaching; and every one said, "Well, now, here is some one who has something to say"; and they filled his church, as men always fill the church of a preacher who is not coaxing and teasing and trying to persuade them to go to church, but who gives them something to go for. They came and heard him, and heard him gladly; and he was really an epoch-making man. "He founded no sect," you say. Well, why should he have founded a sect? What did we want of another sect? Were there not too many sects then, as there are now? Ought we not to be thankful, when we begin to see the end of one of them? Channing founded no sect; but he became easily the leader of a still increasing company of men, who may be said — and we say it reverently — to be of the mind of Jesus; to see God as he saw him; to see men as he saw them, with the same faith: to share his great blessed trusts, his great blessed confidences that this world and the world to come are ours, if we choose to have them, — men who have a blessed Christian optimism, men who have a realistic faith that the kingdom of heaven belongs here on the earth, and that, if we ever mean to get into the kingdom of heaven, we must get into it now. [Applause.] That was his faith, and that was what he preached. I do not mean that he was always conscious of this. He illustrates singularly one of Cromwell's great sayings, that a man never climbs so high as when he does not know where he is going. I do not think Channing knew where he was going, but he was always enlarging, always spreading out. He believed that everything in this life is sacramental, that everything can be made the bread and the wine of a divine life. And so he found sacraments everywhere, and he found subjects to which he could apply his Christianity; and he did apply it far and wide.

Although his knowledge of men was so largely intuitive and inspirational, somehow he did get a most practical knowledge of practical things, and he became a leader of a great company of preachers. You do not find them, happily, set apart in a little sect, but you find them in all sects.

Why, when Dean Stanley was in this country, a little more than a year ago, one of his inquiries was, "Where is the Cemetery of Mount Auburn?" The gentleman to whom he put that question was the Rev. Phillips Brooks. He put it with a great deal of interest. Said Mr. Brooks: "What do you care about Mount Auburn?" For, my friends, it is only one of our cemeteries. We do not take people out there so long as they are living. Said Dean Stanley, "Channing is buried there." He wanted to go out and see Channing's burial-place.

And so you find men everywhere preaching Channing. Channing is preached to-day in pulpits to which, I am afraid, he would hardly now be admitted, for reasons which are doubtless satisfactory to those who so appoint. I make no criticisms upon them. Every man must answer all these things to his own conscience. But it is a fact that he is everywhere preached, because his spirit is abroad.

And so, though I may seem to have spoken lightly of his books, it is not that I think little of them. Their lines have gone out, and are going out wider and wider; but you cannot put such a life as that into any book. It is an ever-unfolding mind. It is an ever-proceeding spirit. It comes in new forms, in new expressions, every day. You think you have got the whole of it, and you find that it is doing a greater work than you ever thought of, and that it has only begun its career. And so I say that he is first, last, always, everywhere, to me, the preacher of this blessed gospel of the Son of God.

In this simple truth,—unformulated, if you choose to use such a word,—as it came from the lips of that blessed and wonderful One, who lived in God, and for God, and for God's children, let us live, and we shall say, as time goes on, in the power and sweetness of this spirit, "The day of Pentecost is fully come." The disciples shall wait no longer in Jerusalem, amid its mingled shadows and light. We mean to know what Jesus says; and his Word is in us, as he said it would be in them. It will be something more than a quotation. We shall know it ourselves, and shall be able to utter it; and then we shall be fit to preach it. We shall have it straight from him. We mean to be as Christian as his disciples were. We do not mean to interpret Jesus by Paul or by John: we mean to interpret Paul and John by Jesus. We mean to get at the reality. That was what Channing sought; and that was what, according to the measure of his age and time and ability he found.

So, while we take some little satisfaction as a denomination in such a man, we rather choose to belong to the greater company,— to be of all those who, with him, are striving to walk in the one light and to build upon the one foundation; and we believe that, if we do it in his spirit, there will be as little as may be of the wood and the hay and the stubble that will be consumed, and as much as may be of that fine gold which the fire can only purify, until it shall be laid up as treasure at God's right hand.

I am very glad to find that so many, this day, have shown that they are of Channing's spirit; and I do not care how much they may be careful to say to me that they do not agree with him in this and that. Well, who does? And who could find out, without a great deal of trouble, precisely what he thought about this or that? And who would care to find out? It is the man's spirit, that ever-proceeding life, in which we rejoice. [Applause.]

The CHAIRMAN. — You have all heard of the Rev. Robert Collyer, formerly of Chicago, but now, I am happy to say, of New York. He is accustomed to speak to full houses, and he must feel at home here. He will please introduce himself.

REMARKS OF REV. ROBERT COLLYER.

Mr. Chairman and Friends,— I do not know when I have felt more like sitting still and enjoying myself, and letting somebody else do the talking. We used to have a saying in our Methodist class-meetings, when we could not say anything else to save us, "It is good to be here." I would like to say just that, and then sit down. At our morning meeting, I got so full that I had to go away; and now I feel so full that I am afraid I shall be like one of those bottles that are so full to the stopper that the water cannot get out!

But I was thinking last night and this morning, and again just now, about something I read once about Channing: that if you went to him, and began to praise him — to praise the man — for something he had said or done, his wonderful eyes seemed to empty themselves of concern, and his face of the beautiful, eager interest, and it would seem to the speaker as if you should talk to the snow of its whiteness or to the fresh west wind of its power of refreshing. He did not like to be praised to his face; and I have felt very glad, in every address that has been made, to notice a certain delicacy of touch about it all,— a feeling, evidently, in the heart of the speaker, like that which Charles Lamb had, who said, I remember, "When we talk about those who have left us, to praise them, we should be as modest as we would if they were still with us on the earth." I have rejoiced in this feeling, which has evidently prevailed in these meetings, — the realization that we must speak with a certain delicacy, with a certain sense of the presence of the man among us, and not overpass the mark so that the praise shall sink into adulation. I feel sure that Channing now, where he dwells, and as he is, cannot have that feeling about all this which he would have, if he were with us still in the flesh; but, if he can be conscious of the words that are uttered to-day all over the world, about his life, in praise of him, he has risen so high and grown so great in that life into which he has gone, that any such words as are said do not trouble him, but he simply takes them and gives them up to the Giver of the gift that made him so great and so good, and in some sweet, spiritual fashion says again what he learned to say as he nestled by his mother's knee,— that beautiful ascription,

"Thine is the kingdom and the power and the glory, forever and ever, Amen." We shall not hurt him by such words as we say, especially as they are said out of such a heart as we witnessed this morning, in that grand meeting in the Church of the Saviour.

But I have felt, sir, all the time, as if any word I might say during these meetings would take, possibly, a different turn from such words as I have heard, noble, beautiful, grand, and sweet as they have been. I have rather longed for some man to say, more emphatically and more incisively, what I recognize in Channing as his grand, broad radicalism, — his deep sympathy with the wide differences as well as the wide agreements of men.

I have been very much interested in the study of Channing's life for years now; and I confess frankly, sir, that this is what has always gone most warmly to my heart: that, while I felt that I could recognize in Channing that beautiful and noble quality of the preacher about which our brother has just spoken so well, there was this also in him, that he had a perpetual sympathy with all sorts of thinkers on all sorts of subjects, and wanted all the time, if he could, to get down into their mind to explore it, to see what good reason lay in them for their conclusion, and so to come into the closest possible sympathy with them, while he must be the man he was in his own convictions and in his own life.

I notice therefore that he, as a young man, with his life before him, had great sympathy for the writings of men like Godwin and Rousseau, and for the writings of Mary Wollstonecraft, who was, he said, one of the greatest women on the earth. And all through his life those who were drawn to him, who gathered about him, who would come to him for help or direction or sympathy, were very much, I think, like those who gathered about David in the old days, in the cave of Adullum. Those who were discontented, and those who were distressed, and I guess, also, those who were in debt,—all kinds of poor creatures,— came to him to get some word that would cheer them, and help them to go forth on special missions in this world, and tell the truth according to such light as might shine forth on their way. I like that quality in Channing,—that grand sympathy for the differences of men in their thinkings and in their conclusions. And I notice that, as he grows older, he loses none of this. It is all in him fresh and true to the last. Some man said to him, I remember, when he was far on in years for him, after he had come through one of the many fights into which he was perpetually plunged, "You seem to be the youngest man in the crowd." "Always young for freedom," he said. It was the deepest thing in his heart, that he should stand by the most absolute freedom of thought and word to which a man can attain.

Robert Hall said of a man, in his day, that his mind was hung on hinges, so that he was always in motion, but made no progress. It was not so with Channing. He was always moving onward to those heights of thought and exploration that made him the grand companion of all the prophets of every name. He gave his heart to the whole truth; and that was the reason why he won so many hearts. I remember he says that for the first twelve years of his ministry he does not remember that he mentioned any sect in the Christian church by name for criticism. He did not want to question and bring into court any of the great religious bodies about him. He always wanted to tell the truth, and let it go home and rest there, and do its work. He had the same feeling towards all sides. Let him find an honest man,—one he believed to be sincere to the bottom of his heart,—and then, so far as he could give that man companionship and sympathy, that man was his friend and his companion. I love that quality in the man. I love to find it forever a flame in his heart. I love to note it as one of the grandest and noblest traits in Channing's character.

Mr. Chairman, in the little village where I lived the better part of my life, three hundred years ago, there were two families, one living on the hill and one in the valley. The family on the hill came there in the time of Henry II. They are there to-day. They have not heard of the Reformation. They are just as nearly as possible what they were at that time, when they went to live there in twelve hundred and something, I do not remember what. The family down in the valley were obscure folk who worked at day's work, and at the time of which I am speaking the representative of the family was earning four cents a day of our present money,— twopence, English. It was borne in upon this working man that this would never do. Something stirred in his heart to strike for a better life; and so at last it came to pass, after another hundred years, they migrated to this New World, leaving the family still on the hill. They were planted down in this soil. They grew, through the grand opportunities that come to a man when he comes from the Old World to the New, somewhere down in the wilds of Maine; and at last they bloomed out into the family of Longfellows, of which we have the poet, and our grand good friend, Sam Longfellow, a minister of our church in Germantown, Pennsylvania. The old family stays on the hill still; but this new one moved onward, and has caught this new life, and has made it noble and beautiful before the world, because there was this fine daring in them to go onward, while the old family remained still in the old family nest.

That was also, in the deeper spiritual sense, the truth with our Channing. He, migrating from the old fastnesses to the new, has made it nobler and more beautiful to those who have to live in it. It was because of this that he became the man he was. It is because of this that we love him and revere him, and speak of him with this affection as we gather together to-night. He was the apostle of a new and nobler life; and it was sufficient to him that under God he was able to do his day's work in his short day.

Shall I say that I love him also for this? I notice sick men are like sick cats: they like to go into a corner, and be let alone. They do not like the movement of their time. They cease to grow aggressive. Everything may go as it will, but they do not want to be bothered. Channing was a sick man. From the time he came from the South, you know, to the time he died, he did not know what it was to be strong, and stand the racket of every day like a man such as our friend Mr. Beecher, for instance. [Applause.] And yet, with that delicate frame, all the time wondering what he should eat and what he should drink and wherewithal he should be clothed, having in this very constitution and make of him conditions of creeping away out of active life, and being quiet somewhere in a corner, and getting off his sermons, some such sermons as our friend described just now, in which everybody will feel good and everybody will be peaceful, and go home and say, "What a capital sermon!" and care nothing at all about it,—a man with such a constitution, we would think, would drive in that direction; but he gave his heart and he gave his life utterly, regardless of the pain, of the fatigue, of the work, of the wear and tear of it, to those great purposes for which God had sent him into the world.

I told them last Sunday, when I was talking about him, that I used to have a coat of Channing's. It went up in the fire, as nearly all things did in Chicago. He gave it to Conant, and Conant left it to me at his death. It was the coat of a boy. "How in the world," I said, "did you manage to do such a grand work on earth with that poor, lean body of yours?" If I ever do take to worshipping a saint, I am going to worship Channing. It is this that draws me to him,—that with his poor chance of doing anything he should have done so much.

Brother Ellis said, just now, that Dr. Chauncy was one of the grand men of the former days; and I was reminded of an anecdote that I read about him, that he wrote one of those progressive books in the direction of the doctrine of Universalism, and hid it in his desk, and durst not bring it out to daylight. Channing never wrote a word that he did not show to the world, no matter what folks might have to say; and he did find those that were not in the heartiest sympathy with him in Boston. There he stood, four-square, —if you can apply such a term as four-square to such a little body,—to every wind that blew, and let them blow and blow, and fought his battle, and then, like a brave man, thought less of what he had done than any other man on earth. Ah! we may well think tenderly of him, and we may well think with pride of him.

And now, Mr. Chairman, ladies and gentlemen, I want to say one word more; and that is, through this great, free soul, we are freer to-day, far and wide. That is a nobler thought; and I trust we will all think more nobly, and, because he has lived, we can all live better.

Our dear friend, in his speech just now, spoke, you know, of Channing's being above, and in a great measure aloof from, what he himself had done; that his sermons were but one part of the grand work, and might not by himself be considered to be at all so grand as many consider them to be now. It reminded me of a day which came once when I got, I was going to say, aggravated, reading a poem of somebody in Philadelphia, which bears the title "No Sect in Heaven." The aggravation arose out of this, that I did not find Unitarians there in any shape whatever. There were the Baptists and the Methodists, the Episcopalians and the Quakers; but there were no Unitarians. And I said, "I am going to make an improvement on that," very much as the Yorkshire man thought he could make an improvement on the Lord's Prayer by making it read, "O Lord, give us this day our daily bread, and some cheese." [Laughter.] I said, "I will write something for the Unitarians"; and this is what I got off. I remember after having got them all in heaven safe and sound, as the other poem got them, I jotted down these lines:—

> Then one came, saying, with low, sweet voice:
> "I have sermons here: they'd the world rejoice.
> I must bear them on to the shining shore,
> And make joy in heaven for evermore."
> But, as twilight is lost in the springing day,
> Doctrine and dogma melted away,
> And Dr. Channing cared no more
> For the word he had said on the time-bound shore.
> And Parker said, "I have sermons seven,
> That must be read in the courts of heaven."
> But the sermons seven went down like lead
> In the waters that run between living and dead.

[Applause.]

The CHAIRMAN.— Rev. Dr. Pullman, of the Sixth Universalist Church in New York, will say a few words to you now.

REMARKS OF REV. J. M. PULLMAN, D.D.

Mr. Chairman, Ladies, and Gentlemen,—If it ever happens to you to be called upon to apologize for not being somebody else, you will be able to enter into my feelings at this moment. I am an eleventh-hour man; and I am here because Dr. Chapin is sick and cannot come. But, finding myself in so brilliant a presence, I suppose I must act by the law of contraries; and, since I cannot speak at all like Dr. Chapin, I must speak as differently from him as I can,—and

I can assure you it is very easy for me not to speak like Dr. Chapin. And I would not be here, honorable as I esteem this position, if I did not know how sorry the Doctor is that he cannot be here; how interested he is in this meeting, how he loved the subject of it, and how all the throbs of his great heart are towards this house to-night. Under the circumstances, I feel that I ought to stand up here and say my Universalist word of praise, whether I say it very well or not.

I labor under an embarrassment in trying to say that word here to-night. I feel as I were between Scylla and Charybdis. I loved Channing very deeply and very dearly; and I loved him for the very things that the world at his time did not love him for. And how shall I, in an assembly like this, gathered from all churches, of all shades of opinion, in beautiful amity and accord, go on and praise him for those things that I love him for, and not jar some discordant note? It would be better for me, doubtless, not to say anything about those matters; and yet, if I speak about a man who loved the truth as he did, and who taught me, in my little way, to love it, I must say what I think. So I am between the Unitarian Scylla and the Orthodox Charybdis.

You know we live in the days when something that is called the "Channing influence" has broadened out, and deepened, and sharpened down into — what shall I say, and be respectful and nice as I would like to be? — I will only say that it has come to something that was in that young gentleman who threw his Euclid aside the other day, because the propositions were too dogmatically stated. He said that he really thought he had a right to doubt whether there was that equality in the angles of an equilateral triangle which the author insisted so much upon.

A general adviser of mankind, who has broken out down East of late years, and broken out very well, — and who advises very well, too, — has said, recently, that by putting his ear to the ground he can hear the retreating footsteps of Channing's influence, or words to that effect. Of course, I must be careful here. I know where the rock is, here and there; but I cannot help saying, men and brethren, that it cannot be very difficult for one who commits himself to the statement that Channing's influence is waning to put his ear to the ground. [Laughter.] If Channing's influence is not making as much stir in the world to-day as it seemed to be making thirty or forty or fifty years ago, it is for the same reason that the water that comes up through my house to the cistern in the attic does not make a noise after a while,—it is because the tank is full; and if Channing's influence does not seem to be as extensive as it was in the earlier days, if it seems to be departing from that level and going downward, it is for the same reason that the water of the reservoir up here sometimes departs from its level, and goes down through a million pipes, and is feeding a million households. I stand for the perpetuity of the influence which I feel so clearly in myself.

If one should ask me what I think is the thing for which William Ellery Channing will be remembered and loved and enshrined among the world's few great men, I should take the broadest generalization I am to make, and say, It is because he taught men to think nobly of God by thinking nobly of themselves. No man that does not think nobly of God can act nobly; and, the more nobly men are taught to think of God, the more nobility you will find in their daily conduct. Is it not so? And is it not true that Dr. Channing himself said, in the preface to one of his published works, that, among all the things there written down, there was this one above all others,— his confidence in the essential worth of human nature, and his disposition to stand up for human liberty? And men thought, "Why, if you elevate the character of men, if you make them think too well of themselves, by so much you lower God." They seemed to think that, in order to get contrast enough, you must make men abject, prone upon their faces, and that then God will be better pleased. Men and brethren of all churches, and of no church, it does not turn out so. Those men who have been taught to feel their own moral ability, and who have been taught to know that of themselves they can do right, are the men that think nobly and speak nobly of God in all churches, and everywhere.

I want to say, before I close, that, so dearly do I prize what has sometimes been called the dogmatism of Channing, I wish it might go further. I do love to see such a spectacle in imagination as some happy people saw in reality in that church in Baltimore, when he preached his famous sermon at the ordination of Jared Sparks. It must have been grand to have seen that slight, pale man, with deep eyes that looked through all things, and to have heard him say: "We all agree externally, do we not, upon the character of God,—as to his goodness, as to his holiness, and as to his power? Yes: externally we do; but it is possible to speak magnificently of God, and to think very meanly of him,—to apply high-sounding epithets to God personally, and to apply principles to his government that are odious." And then he went on to describe the reasons why he loved and trusted and worshipped God,—that he did it not simply because God had power, but because that power was good, and was exerted for good; not because he was a Ruler only, but because he was a good Ruler. And then came that grand sentence, which I know I shall never forget,—"We respect nothing but excellence on earth or in heaven." Am I wrong, men and brethren, when I say that in the development of the intellectual and spiritual life of Channing he grew toward the Christ, and not away from him? Have I erred in drawing from his words those thoughts that seem to me to indicate that, the longer and the more closely he looked, the more dearly he loved the Lord and Saviour Jesus Christ? I may be mistaken,—I know upon what rock I am running,—but I believe that from my heart and soul.

So I speak for the Universalist Church, who see in Channing the exemplification of that which they consider their central light and doctrine, of the moral perfection of the Almighty. The corollary which follows from this is the final extinction of moral evil; and, taking him as one of those who has contributed so largely to a result everywhere so desirable and noble, how can I better close this short address than in the words of Dean Stanley, as quoted for us from Norman Macleod, speaking from the general aspect of the man? "A man broad with the breadth of the charity of Almighty God, and narrow with the narrowness of his righteousness." [Applause.]

The assembly then rose and sang, as before, the following selected hymn : —

> Come, kingdom of our God,
>   Sweet reign of light and love;
> Shed peace and hope and joy abroad,
>   And wisdom from above.
>
> Over our spirits first
>   Extend thy healing reign;
> There raise and quench the sacred thirst
>   That never pains again.
>
> Come, kingdom of our God,
>   And make the broad earth thine;
> Stretch o'er her lands and isles the rod
>   That flowers with grace divine.
>
> Soon may all tribes be blest
>   With fruit from life's glad tree;
> And in its shade like brothers rest,
>   Sons of one family.

The CHAIRMAN.— I now have the honor to present to you the Hon. George William Curtis. [Applause.]

ADDRESS OF MR. CURTIS.

Mr. President, Ladies, and Gentlemen,— As a son of Rhode Island, I have peculiar pride and pleasure in this day. My native State is small, but it is rich in great memories and in great men. The stone of religious liberty, which my Brother Ellis's Massachusetts rejected, became the head of the corner in Rhode Island; and upon the foundation principle of that little State is reared the vast superstructure of the civil and religious liberty of America.

And look with me, for an instant, at the contributions of Rhode Island to American history. In our earliest epoch, it gave us Roger Williams, its founder,— the preacher, not of religious tolerance, but of absolute religious liberty, who held that the Quaker and the Puritan who hung the Quaker, that George Fox and John Endicott, were both of them too narrow for the broad church of soul-liberty. To the Revolution, Rhode Island gave General Greene, the friend of Washington, and Esek Hopkins, the first Commodore, the first Commander-in-chief, of the American Navy. To the later war with Britain, Rhode Island gave Commodore Perry, who upon Lake Erie met the enemy, and they were his. And, last of all, my native State gave to America and the world, to liberty and to humanity, William Ellery Channing. [Applause.]

Among the thousand tributes of reverence and of love that are to-day paid to his memory, I have been asked to say to you a word of his anti-slavery career. Why, Mr. President, there is not a man who shall speak of him who will not speak of that. Every breath he drew was an anti-slavery inspiration. Every word he uttered was an anti-slavery battle. Wherever he saw a chain binding the human soul or the human body, he struck it, and he broke it,— not with the might of the trip-hammer that shatters, but with the touch of the sunbeam that melts.

Channing was one of the three great spiritual emancipators in our history. The first was Roger Williams; the second was Channing; the third, in a later generation, was Ralph Waldo Emerson. [Applause.] They all held to what Roger Williams called "soul-liberty." They all asserted that moral independence was the sole source of moral power; that the moment any man looked for his duty to the platform of a party, or to the creed of a sect, or to any authority, to any source, but his own conscience, which is God in him, that moment he lost his moral liberty. And, sir, I rejoice to see this great and brilliant assembly, at a time when every mind in the country is forecasting the vast excitements of the Presidential election, when passions and ambitions, and hopes and prejudices of every kind, are fiercely inflamed. The serene memory of a man like Channing falls upon us like a benediction of manly courage and peace. For so long, fellow-citizens, as we are true to his principles; so long as, in a country of sects and parties, we hold them as servants, and not as masters; so long as we trample under our feet the familiar ecclesiastical, the familiar political sophistries, scorning their scorn, despising their contempt, excommunicating their excommunications,— so long we shall understand the mysterious saying that one with God is a majority; and our beloved country will be truly invincible because truly free.

The supreme passion of Channing's life—if I may use such a word to describe a man so passionless, or, rather, who held all his powers and passions under so strict control— was love of liberty. To him God was perfect love and perfect freedom. It was this which made him intensely individual, and it was this which gave him his profound sense of the worth of man as man.

He lived in a time of tremendous controversies,—political, theological, social. He was always a teacher of the teachers, a leader of the leaders; but he bore himself throughout with absolute heroism and independence, always serene, superior, solitary. His manner was as gentle and sweet as the dew that falls on Hermon; but his convictions, rooted upon the Eternal Centre, were as absolutely uncompromising as the mountain upon which the dews of Hermon fall. And as to-day we look back into that stormy time, as we catch a glimpse of that slight figure and seraphic glance amid the heavings of the tempestuous epoch, amid the contentions of statesmen, of politicians, of theologians, of reformers, we seem to see a fervent and penetrating flame that purifies while it illuminates; and we catch at least some glimpse of that essential and innate dignity of human nature which was his profound faith, and the theme of his transcendent eloquence.

Mr. President, I can hardly believe, as I look around upon this audience, that there are so many who honor me at this moment with their attention, so many young men and so many young women who have no personal remembrance of our great anti-slavery debate. It was a question which involved a wrong against human nature, a crime against liberty, so immense and so intolerable that it necessarily overshadowed all other questions; and if I have given you, in the few words that I have spoken, my idea of the golden key that unlocks the whole career of Channing, you will understand where a man, arrayed by the very law of his nature against despotism, necessarily stood in that great conflict. The question was absolutely unavoidable. Ah! sir, I speak to men who remember with me how we sought to escape it. I speak to men who remember how we evaded the omnipresent issue, how we said that it belonged to the South; that it was so "nominated in the bond," that it was not our affair, that we were morally free from taint. Why, human slavery, as it existed in this country, was a cancer which could live only by tainting the sound flesh around it; and, by the very law of its being, slavery within the Union necessarily encroached upon freedom within the Union. It was everywhere. It was not to be evaded. Beyond the Mississippi, the free laborer, planting his happy home and singing at his work in the free territory, suddenly found himself confronted by the spectre of slavery, in the persons of the overseer and his gang, to dispute with slaves the bread of freedom.

It was not beyond the Mississippi alone; but the panting fugitive, guilty of no crime but color, taking his life in his hand, tracked by blood-hounds, suffering torments which have not been written, and following his only friend, the cold north star in heaven, fled across the border, and here, in your very Brooklyn streets, cowering and starving and knocking upon your own doors, brought home to you, at your hearthstone, the crime and the appalling sorrow of slavery.

Nor on the land alone, but on the sea,—far out on the ocean, beyond the sight of land,—innocent men, overpowering other men who, for their own gain only, had robbed them of their liberty, were obliged to go somewhere to shore, and, coming to our coast, piteously appealed to the protection of our flag; and the government which that flag symbolized hesitated and demurred. But let me say it to the eternal honor of a man then living, an ex-President of the United States, whose heart and mind echoed the pitiful cry that he heard, personally a friend of Channing, and also of the religious faith of Channing, but with the ability, with the instinct of a moral gladiator, that he, virtually alone in Congress, with his strong hand and his dauntless will upheld American liberty in the House of Representatives, maintained for us the fundamental American principle of the right of petition, and in the Supreme Court of the United States made the poor foreign slaves, the slaves of the "Amistad," his clients, and gave them liberty.

When I think of this man, I see John Pym in the Commons, thundering against Charles Stuart; I see Lord Mansfield upon the King's Bench, declaring that there cannot be a slave in England: and I feel that, in the darkest hour of American history, America and human liberty had no truer friend than John Quincy Adams. [Applause.]

Well, this was the contest with which Channing was confronted. There was not a man in this country who could feel the crime more deeply than he, and you will see at once that two things were to be expected of him. He would be one of the earliest and most intrepid of the anti-slavery leaders, and he would not be identified with the party known as abolitionists. On reading our history, you will find that both of these facts are verified by the record.

Channing, by temperament, by the intense individuality of which I have spoken, represents everywhere the individual force, the individual influence. His refinement, his sensitiveness of temperament, and his overpowering sense of justice made him, more than any man in the country, alive to what he conceived to be the excesses and the personalities of reform.

Now, fellow-citizens, I do not read Channing aright, if it was the bitterness of invective, so much as what seemed to him its injustice, which kept him solitary in the great awakening. He had no personal aim. He had no private ambition. All his ends were God's, his country's and truth's,—these and nothing more. His object was always a moral object. It was persuasion; and therefore he recoiled from vituperation, and denounced it, as defeating the very object of the reform. Whatever made persuasion, in his judgment, impossible, was to him a flagrant crime against the cause, and a betrayal of the slave himself.

But, on the other hand, the abolitionists, viewing this question with their conscience, with their knowledge of mankind, with their experience of daily affairs, considered moderation treachery. They regarded Channing as a man who compromised, and who might even be accused of cowardice. But Samuel J. May, one of those saintly souls akin to Channing's, early caught up in the ardor of this great crusade of humanity, tells us that Channing, always open, always generous, as Mr. Collyer has said, to every claim of every man and of every cause, asked him perpetually how that cause was coming on, and one day reproved Mr. May for what he considered to be the extravagance of reform. Mr. May tells us that he at once responded, "Well, Dr. Channing, God works with such instruments as he can find. He has called the world, he has called the mighty, he has called the leaders of men, and they have not answered. We have come in from the hedges and from the ditches, we have come in from the highways and by-ways, and are here to do our work. Look to it, sir, look to it; for the work in the Master's vineyard will be surely done. Is it not time, sir, that you spoke?" Mr. May said that the moment he had uttered this reproof to Channing he sat drooping before him, not knowing what the rebuke might be; but Channing, with the utmost simplicity, answered: "Brother May, I feel the justice of that reproof. I have kept silence too long."

I do not, for myself, think that he had kept silence in an unjust sense. Every word, every act of his, had been charged with the anti-slavery spirit; and of his great co-laborer, William Lloyd Garrison [applause], and Dr. Channing,—both residents of the same city, both moved by the same inspiration, both pursuing the same end, but absolutely different in temperament and training,—all we can say is, as of all the resplendent planets in the great heaven of that agitation, "One star differeth from another star in glory."

For, from the beginning, when Channing was born, a hundred years ago to-day in Newport, Newport was a slave-trading port. Its public opinion was what the public opinion of New York was when the anti-slavery agitation began. Down to the period just before the war, the public opinion of New York was expressed by one of its greatest merchants, when he said, "There will be no peace in this country until men like Charles Sumner are hung." In that one remark, those who were not familiar with those days may understand what those days were.

Well, in the old Newport in which Channing was born, his first preacher, in the church to which his father went, was old Dr. Hopkins, who preached every Sunday the terrors of hell to a poor congregation in a desolate church, and who insisted to them that the final test of true faith was the willingness to be damned for the glory of God. [Laughter.] Old Dr. Hopkins, preaching that faith, was still a worthy embassador of Him who came to break every bond. And it was from his lips, from his life, and from the whole adverse stress of public opinion there in Newport, that Dr. Channing first acquired his hostility to slavery as it existed in this country.

Then, when he is eighteen years of age, just at the very beginning of the century, he goes to Richmond to teach. And he writes home from Richmond, "Except for their sensuality and their slavery,"—two considerable exceptions,—"the Virginians would be the finest people in the world."

In 1830, when Garrison began his *Liberator* Dr. Channing was in Santa Cruz for his health. But in Santa Cruz, amid all the delights of Elysium, he could see and feel but one thing. Like the princess in the fairy tale who could not sleep upon a hundred beds of down because of the little pebble under them all, so he could not rejoice in all the splendor and prosperous luxuriance of the tropics, knowing the injustice to human nature that was beneath its whole social system.

When he returned to Boston, he stood in the pulpit of a congregation panoplied in as obdurate a respectability against every form of agitation of the anti-slavery question as any congregation in the land. Yet he did not hesitate to say, as he stood meekly before them, "I have been in Santa Cruz. I have seen in Santa Cruz the mildest form of human slavery; and in its mildest form, brethren, human slavery is the destroyer of the soul."

In 1835 and in 1837, he published his essay upon Slavery, and his letter upon Texas to Henry Clay. I challenge for those two documents the merit of being the most permanent and imperishable contributions to the literature of the anti-slavery cause, as expressing its fundamental reason and principle and scope.

I do not forget for a moment — how could I in this presence? — the words of the prophet, and the John Knox of that movement, of whom I have already spoken, Mr. Garrison. [Applause.] I do not forget the mingled trumpet and flute of the speech of Phillips, which has so often filled this very building with the truest music of eloquence. [Applause.] I do not forget that great appeal, that romance, in which the whole life of slavery was figured, which was borne into every land, which was translated into every language, and which melted the heart of the world, as it pondered the career of "Uncle Tom." [Applause.] I do not forget that, as Emerson said, in every anti-slavery meeting the eloquence was dog-cheap. But the plea of Channing, perfectly tranquil in tone, stands, it seems to me, always separate and apart. These were his words: "God has not intrusted the reform of the world to passion." His argument was a calm and permanent statement. It is the argument which our children's children will read, and feel to be invincible. It will not have the glow, the fervor, the palpitation of the speeches and the appeals to which our hearts have responded; but it will shine always with the calm light of the stars.

Nor was he wanting — I think my best anti-slavery friends will acknowledge — in his fidelity to his profound conviction. The work of our friend Mr. Oliver Johnson — the last contribution to the history of the anti-slavery reform — tells us that it was not until 1843 that Mr. Garrison felt called upon to declare his gospel of the dissolution of the Union, because it was then his feeling that the Union was a covenant with death and an agreement with hell. But in the essay upon Slavery, eight years before, and in his letter to Mr. Clay, five years before, Dr. Channing had done what every man in this country was warned by the statesmen not to do, — he had weighed the value of the Union; and he had said: "To other men the Union is a means, but to me it is an end. I love the Union with a love surpassing all the feeling that I have for any American institution but that of liberty." "We will make every concession for the Union," said Channing, "but truth, justice, and liberty: these we will not concede." And when he wrote to Clay in 1837, he did not hesitate to speak of the consummation of the annexation of Texas as a justification for the separation of these States. With celestial prescience, he knew that the States could not cohere, slave and free. He knew that they would separate either by the sword or by consent; and, as a man of peace, he hoped that it might be by consent. And, when he said these words, he seems to me to have repeated those great words of Burke, — "All government is founded upon compromise and barter; but in every bargain the thing sold must bear some proportion to the price paid. No man will barter away the immediate jewel of his soul." Channing spoke the deepest conviction of the American people before they knew it themselves. He spoke for that love of liberty, for that fidelity to the Union, which, when the trial came, was sure to be found supreme. When our Southern brethren made their demand, they asked us to barter away the immediate jewel of our soul. They have had their answer.

Mr. President, many voices in many lands are at this moment speaking of this man. He is shown in a hundred aspects. I have mentioned one. But turn this priceless diamond in your hand; and, wherever you look, every smooth facet will be as pure and luminous as every other.

I never saw Channing, I never heard his voice; but, walking often in the old Newport garden that he loved, I have felt that its sunny solitude, penetrated by the cool, racy breath and the infinite murmur of the neighboring sea, was the truest symbol of his life and character.

We cannot truly appreciate, nor fitly express, our debt to the great men who are not specialists, who are not — if my brother will allow me — preachers merely, nor reformers, but who are great uplifting powers which supply the thoughts that make civilization, who give us the inspirations that make the glory of our life. These things we cannot express; but our deepest souls and all that is noblest within us respond to them, as the shells strown upon that Newport beach of his answer the eternal music of the ocean.

> "Our echoes roll from soul to soul,
> And grow forever and forever."

The heavenly light in those sweet eyes is long since quenched; the music of that voice is silent; that gentle presence has vanished from men's sight forever; that slight figure, that trembling body, lies mouldering in the grave. But in the greater spiritual liberty that we see, in the quickened public conscience, in the downfall of sectarian divisions, in the deeper, higher, truer sense of the fatherhood of God and the brotherhood of men, that soul of fire and of love goes marching on. [Loud applause.]

The CHAIRMAN.— The Rev. Dr. Sims, of the Methodist Church, will now address you.

ADDRESS BY REV. C. N. SIMS, D.D.

A Californian, with whom his nephew had been long visiting, grew strangely sad. The nephew anxiously inquired the cause of his grief, and was surprised to hear his uncle say, "I am so afraid you will never come to see me again." "I certainly will," said the affectionate young man. "No," said the uncle. "I think you never will, for I am afraid you will never go away this time."

Now, my friends, I do assure you our meeting to-night *will close some time*, so you may have a chance to come again. In view of the lateness of the hour, I promise to be extremely brief. Indeed, I only speak at all, because it is fitting that I, and Mr. Beecher who is to follow me, should put an orthodox finish to this centennial celebration, and that it should pass under orthodox revision, as all such meetings ought.

The world is not rich enough in virtue or strength to permit a great, good man to be forgotten. It has no superabundant accumulation of truth, that we can afford to turn away from any truth-searcher, no matter though his methods be different from ours; and we are here to-night, my friends, to speak words of grateful remembrance of one who was a courageous, devoted searcher after the truth, and who consecrated that truth to the best interests of humanity, as he understood them.

William Ellery Channing is one of the few men who have escaped death and oblivion, and who live on forever in the truest life, because he was a great man, after the Master's deepest and most profound definition of greatness, — being the servant of all. His influence upon the world is twofold. It is impersonal, in so far as it goes out to affect general thought and sentiment. As a rivulet on its way to the river gives its waters to the atmosphere, and then those waters are condensed into dew-drops and deposited upon leaf and flower and bud, and yet are truly of the rivulet, though they may not make their way with it to the river, so there are lives that in their definite and living influence quicken and refresh all humanity, long after they themselves have disappeared from any personality in the matter. But, beside that, there is another influence upon the general thought of the world as we have studied him, the philanthropist, the teacher; the man whose words and thoughts have been before the world, always fresh, never belonging to a departed or to a decayed age; the glorious thinker, searching after truth.

I speak of his continuous personal influence. To the student of his biography, who has followed his labor and struggle and thought, he is still a most living personality, able yet to stir the thought, arouse the enthusiasm, and inspire to noble efforts and purposes. His was the life of a great, consecrated searcher after God's verities. He was a man who gave himself to know the truth. Because the statements of Christian doctrine around him did not satisfy his mind, he sought to make other statements which seemed to him more correct. In order to do his work, he became a great and glorious martyr for the truth as he understood it, willing to part company with old friends, willing to feel whatever pain he may have felt in the disapprobation of those under whom he had been instructed, from whom he had learned, and whom he had loved. He parted company with them for conscience' sake.

And so the student of Channing's character comes to

catch the inspiration of one who loved the truth, not simply to love what Channing believed. If it were that, we could not all mingle here to-night. But we come to stand where he stood, on this broad principle of loving the truth as he loved it, and to judge of the truth for ourselves as he judged of it for himself; and this inspiration is one which must always be healthful and helpful.

Again, the influence of his personal character upon those who study him is felt in his broad, earnest, tender, loving philanthropy. He was a man of generous nature, one who could agree to honor those with whom he disagreed. Not every man can forgive his fellow for holding opinions not in harmony with his own. Many a one can forgive the thief who steals his watch, that cannot pardon his neighbor who fails to find his faith expressed in the same catechism. Because Channing's soul was full of sympathy, he lives largely in my mind and in my affections. It seemed as if his heart was the focal centre of a whispering gallery broad as this wide world; and that every sigh of human woe and every sob of human sorrow came to be articulate and audible, as it reported to his spirit.

So he came to stand before the world the advocate of temperance; the advocate of freedom; the advocate of religion; the man of pure and noble life; the man who loved humanity in its loneliness and poverty; the Sabbath-school man; the pastor who cared for the poor and needy; the man whose broad and loving heart planned all generous things for all men; the man who planned for the emigrant, for the workingman, for the mechanic, for the degraded, for the imprisoned,— planned for whoever suffered or was ignorant or fallen or hopeless in this world,— and who longed to lift up humanity toward the God whom he worshipped. He was a reverent worshipper of God.

This world, my friends, is broad enough, God's love rich

enough, and his character grand enough, for all of us, with our different religious views, to stand on, and gaze straight up into the face of our divine Father, and not be in one another's way. He loved God and believed in him, and he that hath this hope in him purifieth himself even as He is pure; and his whole life grew beautiful in the sunshine of the divine favor and love, and in the light of God's all-seeing eye, with nothing evil hid away in his heart or in his hand. So he gave his life to humanity. So he lives on, having escaped death. So to-day, in all that makes up life, the helper of the thinker and the worker, of the student, and the down-trodden, he lives on. The life of flesh is past. He does not any longer eat and drink, and suffer and toil; but he helps humanity, and he will help it through all the years that are to come. And so, believing, as I do, in the essential divinity of our Lord Jesus Christ, in the permanent and perpetual power of God's Holy Spirit, and in the doctrine and reality of genuine conversion, I come to lay my chaplet down in memory of one whom I honor; and I pray God that all truth gathered everywhere in this wide world may be consecrated to the service of all men, and that all truth-seekers may be honorable in the sight of their brethren forever.

The CHAIRMAN.—Of course you will all remain to hear Mr. Beecher.

ADDRESS OF REV. HENRY WARD BEECHER.

I do not propose to speak to-night at any length. It is now a time at which Dr. Channing would have been abed and asleep for an hour. You have had a banquet, if ever an audience had; and you have also had the benediction of a good sound orthodox clergyman at the end of it. And it seems to me that the consent of men, whether they are in the Mother Church or in any of the scattered sectarian churches, — orthodox, half-orthodox, or heterodox, — is all gained to-night, and gained on one point: that a man who loves God fervently and his fellow-men heartily, and devotes his life to that love, is a member of every communion and of every church, and is orthodox in spite of orthodoxy or anything else!

There is one point, however, that has been pressed upon my mind, as I have been overwhelmed with the richness of the thoughts and illustrations of the speakers gone by. So warm and enthusiastic have been the eulogies to-night, that one might almost imagine that Dr. Channing was himself the light of the world! But no; so rich is God, so all-pervading, so incarnated in every soul that thinks and in every heart that throbs, that Dr. Channing was but one single taper shining in the darkness of this world, and drawing his light from the great solar Fountain, God. He was the mouthpiece of his time; but his time had prepared the material which he expressed. No man, in any age, though he stand head and shoulders above his fellows, is competent to do much more than has been wrought out for him, — to be the teacher of those things which have been made needed, and manifestly needed, by the experience of millions of men, and to give intellectual expression to those truths which in their emotive form have welled up in thousands and tens of thousands of bosoms. Dr. Channing felt all the accumulated force, moral and social, of the times gone by and the times at hand in which he lived. And so, though he was great, mankind behind him was greater, the time was greater, and the all-informing spirit of God was greater yet.

In my boyhood, I went to Boston in 1826, and was thrown into the very centre and heat of that great controversy which was raging, in which my father was an eloquent thunderer on one side, and in which Dr. Channing was an eloquent silent man on the other side. Mostly his work had been done at that time. Do I not remember the image of that day? In my own nature enthusiastic, sincere, and truthful, did not what my father thought become what I thought? And did I not know that Unitarians were the children of the devil? And did I not know that those heresiarchs, if they had not fallen from heaven, ought to fall from the earth? And did I not regard Channing, I will not say as a man misled, but as a man demented, in whom was the spirit of error, leading men down to perdition, and who ought to be silenced, and all of whose followers ought to be scourged? Did I not read in those days the haughty statement, the reply, the rejoinder, and then the diffusive controversy generally? And yet time has wrought with me, as it has wrought with you, and with all men, wonderful changes; and now those two men, my father and Dr. Channing, that stood over against each other,—to my young seeming,—as wide apart as the east from the west, I see standing together, and travelling in precisely the same lines, and toward precisely the same results. For did not Lyman Beecher feel that, as the doctrine of God and of moral government was presented in the day in which he lived, the glory of God was obscured, that men were bound hand and foot, and that the sweetness and the beauty of the love of Christ in the gospel were misunderstood, or even veiled and utterly hidden? And what was he striving for but such a renovation of the old orthodoxy as should let the light of the glory of God, as it shone in the face of Jesus Christ, have a fair chance at folks? And what was Channing striving for? He felt that the old formulas and statements of men did not let out the whole circumference, nor did it give the whole force and beauty of the character of God. He, too, was driving, as best he could, the clouds out of heaven, and seeking to make the character of God more resplendent, and morally more effective to mankind. And there they stood bombarding each other, both of them with the same grand object and motive; like two valiant men-of-war, that are giving each other broadside after broadside, and yet are on a stream of Providence that is carrying them unconsciously in the same direction! They sailed side by side, and as they met in heaven I think they lifted up hands of wonder and exclaimed, "Is it possible that I am here — and you?"

My estimate of Channing is not less because my estimate of the whole force of society is greater. He was *one* of the men, and but one, — a great and noble and leading man. Ten thousand other things were working. When Sisera was at his battle, the stars in their courses, it is said, fought against him; and, when God hath great work on hand, the stars, and everything that is beneath them, are working in one direction. The changes in governments, the advance in laws, the development of a better political economy, the evolution of commonwealths, the progress of science and of the mechanic arts, but especially the science of mind, are working out a final theology by working to the same great end, — the emancipation of man, the clarity of his understanding, the sovereignty of his conscience, the sympathies of his soul, and the full disclosure of God, over all, blessed forever. And it is enough glory to say of Channing that he understood the day in which he lived, and understood that he was appointed to be a pilot to the times that were to come after; and that whatever he did administratively he did intelligently, that the young and the vital wood that carried the sap and the life of the tree might have a chance.

Those who are horticulturists will understand that the bark that carried the sap last year will have to get out of the way, and let the bark that comes on this year have a chance; and the kind pomologist, with his knife, often slits the bark of the cherry-tree that is conservative, to give a chance to that which has a hereditary right to be the bark, and let the bark-bound diameter of the tree expand a little. Dr. Channing, among other men, used his knife for the sake of letting the new truth, which was struggling for a larger diameter in the world, have a chance.

Well, what has been the result? That was one hundred years ago to-day. And what would Channing think if he were allowed to stand here to-night? He would have been half deaf by this time, if he had heard every thing that has been said on this platform; but, if he turned his eye upward, and saw the change that has come over the American world, to say nothing of Christendom, during the last hundred years, and contrasted the spirit of antipathy which existed between sect and sect, between theologian and theologian, and the spirit which exists between them now, what would be his thought? Even so sympathetic a man as my father never saw an Arminian come into his church in that early day, that he did not feel bound to give him such a dose of Calvinism as would physic him for a year! I know very well how stringent were the habits, the methods, the peculiarities of each sect, and how each sect defended itself. They were like so many nests of wasps in neighboring trees, each one stinging for his own nest, and each one fighting against the nest of every other.

So the fiery sects, if they were not dead and buried in worldliness, or when they revived and came to life, were animated by a spirit of antipathy and suspicion and jealousy. Of course the spirit of envy and jealousy is universal and continuous; but in that early day there was the spirit of criticism and of suspicion, and it all sprang from a very obvious source. For had they not embraced that world-wide heresy, that God had committed his kingdoms in this world to the consciences of his official disciples, and had ordained their consciences to govern the consciences of all mankind? Has it not been the bane of every sect, from the beginning to this day, that men have felt that they were the special depositaries of divine knowledge, and that the deposition gave them the power to dictate to other men what they should think and what they should believe, and to hold the rod of everlasting damnation over their head, if they did not think and believe as they were told? All men held substantially this view then, and some men hold it even now. So it came to pass that each sect followed its own notion of God, marking out exactly the line of the wall, throwing up exactly the right bulwarks, and defending what each man knew to be the one exclusive truth of creation, and feeling bound to look sharp at all the others, to contest them, and to condemn them, that the deposit of truth which each one had in purity might have a fair chance in this world!

That is all changed. I remember when you could not get a minister of the Episcopal Church, and of the Unitarian, and of the Universalist, and of the Swedenborgian, and of the Baptist, and of the Congregationalist, on to a common platform. You could scarcely do it on the Fourth of July, and it was a wonder then that they did not fight. But, to-day, on how many different subjects are they glad to come together and consult! And how marvellous an event is it of the time in which I live, to see all these stanch churches, by their stanchest ministers and advocates, stand together through one long day with nothing on their tongue but praises of that heretic Unitarian, Dr. William Ellery Channing! Time and the world *do* move. Changes *have* been wrought.

And more than that: there has come in, from influences which it has pleased God to give forth and distribute in the heart and understanding of many a man, but by none more than by Channing, a change by which it is understood in this world that, if God is to have all the glory, then he must be represented to be a God that is altogether glorious; that, if he is to have sovereign and absolute control of men, then he is to have sovereign and absolute control of men because all the faculties of the human soul which he infixed in mankind for the very purpose of judging what is right and what is wrong, what is just and what is unjust, what is holy and pure and what is unholy and impure, are satisfied with the representations that are made of him; and the whole Christian world to-day is feeling after such a representation of God as mankind will not let die out. No view of God will be allowed to reign which does not conform to the enlightened moral sense of good men. While there are men who are atheists largely because the God on which they have been fed is not God, is a misrepresentation of the true God, in churches all over our land,—and, with perhaps more reluctant step, in the churches of other lands,—the cry of Christendom is: "Give to us a God that shall not be apologized for! Give to us a God that we do not need to defend! Give to us a God that, when the child, and the mother of the child, and the just man, and the loving soul, look up, they shall say, 'Whom have I in heaven but thee? and there is none that I desire upon earth beside thee.'"

The Calvinistic theology of New England before Channing's day had become intolerable to the best Orthodox men, and Channing was but one of many who sought its modification. Judged by the Scotch, the Genevese standard, Edwards, Hopkins, Bellamy, West, Spring, Backus, Strong, Dwight, and a host of others, were smoothing its features, and softening its immedicable harshness. The revolt against this system of organized fatalism and infinite despotism is not yet ended. In the lecture-room of the schools, where intellect has supreme sway and the heart is excluded, it still lives, but in the pulpit it has perished.

The educated moral sense of the laymen has slain it. The free air of human life, the play of Christian sympathies upon it, have made it as impossible to employ it as it would be to uphold astrology, or alchemy, or the inquisition.

But, while we thus speak of Calvinism, John Calvin was illustrious as a radical. He broke away from the reigning spirit of his times, and led the spirit of free inquiry. Were he alive in our day, no man would scourge Calvinism with such resounding blows as John Calvin! Nor was his theological system without great benefit, in an age when the king and the priest had more power upon the senses and the imagination than God. Men believed in nothing that they could not see and handle. The Church was busy in bringing all high and ineffable truth into a sensuous condition.

Over against this magnificent Rome, with its cathedrals, altars, robed priests, processions, gorgeous ceremonies, filling the eye, and bringing down the spiritual man to the bondage of the senses, Calvin wrought out a theology of thought, logical, elaborate, complete. When men pointed to the visible church, its flowing rituals and its impressive trappings, and asked tauntingly, "Where is your religion? There is ours, visible to all men, sublime and beautiful," Calvin pointed to his system, invisible yet powerful, addressed to reason, not sense; a system that aroused fear, that developed imagination, that moved in men's thoughts as laws of nature move upon the earth. His God was full-orbed in power, and his light and glory extinguished the false lights of the throne and the altar. It was a time when nations were being dashed in pieces as a potter's vessel; and Calvin's God was the very divine iconoclast, going forth to overthrow idols and polluted temples, and drive headlong all usurpers of His prerogatives. His attributes did not shock the rude ideas of that day. It only concentred in God the barbaric authority to which men had wearily and long submitted in magistrates and masters. Better one despot than a thousand. That system, which now oppresses the conscience and shocks the moral sense, in its day emancipated reason, developed the moral sense, and inspired men with ideas that led to liberty in the State and in the Church.

But, like the steel armor of our fathers, admirable in its day, it can be no longer worn. The spirit of God has advanced men beyond the need of such an instrument. It must be placed in the hall, or gathered in military museums, with broadswords, spears, culverins, and the whole panoply of antiquated weapons.

Our age has witnessed, and is still rejoicing in, a better idea of justice. There has been a great advance in our day in the conception of justice, as an emanation of sympathy and love, and not a deification of combativeness and destructiveness. Justice has been made vindictive rather than vindicatory. The principle of hate has ruled in civil law, in government, in theology, and in the churches. We have had a fighting, and not a loving Christianity. Repulsion has been stronger than attraction, dislike than sympathy. Upon this dreary winter, spring is advancing. It has not yet conquered. Here and there come blustering days, to renew the rigor and to destroy this new life. But the Sun of Righteousness is now high in the heavens. The days are longer; the light advances, and the warmth.

All things are tending to draw men to each other. The things in which men agree are more and more important than those in which they differ. Love is growing, hate is weakening.

More than that, I think in the past one hundred years — and this, the birthday of Channing, marks the beginning of it — there has not only been a change in the spirit of sects, in the notions of government and in theology, but there has also been a wonderful progress in true religion. If you measure religion by the exact forms of any of the highly organized churches,— our mother, Rome, and her eldest daughter, the Episcopal Church; if you measure it by dogma and formality and ordinance, in the different aspects in which the denominations present it; if you measure its condition by the Westminster Catechism, or by the Confession of Faith, or by any of the mediæval Confessions, or by the hitherto standing claims of any of the organized religious bodies,— I think it must be admitted that there is a decadence of religion. But how? When the morning star begins to shine, the nimble lamplighters of our cities go around extinguishing one gaslight after another. They were substitutes for daylight; but, when the sun is coming up, there is no longer use for gaslight. And shall any man say, "They are putting out the light of the world"? They are putting out the artificial lights that help up through the night, but are they destroying daylight?

If religion means veneration, there is not so much as there was. Our own institutions do not tend to breed veneration. Our children know as much as we do at fifteen years of age, and govern us at twenty! Our magistrates have but little dignity. We put them up merely that we may pelt them. To nominate a man for office in our land is to stigmatize him; and to elect him is to damn him! There is nothing old in America but trees; and people do not care for them. For it is with us as of old, when a man was accounted great as he lifted up an axe against the trees; and almost nothing in the body politic is sacred in our scrambling, active land, where men are building every one for himself. There is little veneration here; and, if that is religion, Heaven help us! We have tried to breed it. We build big churches with small windows. We put out what little light can get through, with paint. We have imitations of grotesque things that have come down five hundred or one thousand years, and we try to dress as they used to dress before they knew how to dress! In every way possible, we are trying to coax the old mediæval spirit of veneration. We cannot do it: it is not bred in our day. It will not live in our land. The common school is against it; the elective franchise is against it; the whole of our society is against it. So dangerous are the lapses of men now in theology that we are all of us trying to stop that; and we are refurbishing the old armor, and the word is going out: "We must reprint the old doctrines, and we must introduce a shrewder economy in our seminaries, and we must screw up the system. It is getting loose and shackly." The engineers are screwing it up here and there, and by every means striving to make it work as it used to work. There is such a widespread doctrinal defection — with one or two exceptions — that, if you are to measure the progress of religion by the exact agreement of men to confession and catechism, woe be to religion!

Religion is of the heart. It is a living force. Books do not contain it, but only describe it. Creeds and Catechisms may be honored while religion is perishing; and religion may be increasing in scope and sweetness while creeds are waning. It is born in every generation, and in every heart that is a child of God; and one cannot find whether men have religion or not by bringing them to the catechism, or by asking them how they got it. We have learned one thing, and that is that mankind are greater than all the governments of mankind. We have learned that man is more than the church, and that the church was made for man, and not man for the church. We have learned that, if there is such a thing as religion, it is not to be found in any machinery. We have learned that religion is loving God and loving our fellow-men.

Now, then, tested by that, is there more or less religion in the age in which we live than there was in the days that are gone by? I say, more. I call the whole civilized world to witness that, although there is much of the lion, of the bear, of the eagle, and of the vulture yet in mankind, and though these foul beasts or birds float on our national banners and represent much of the under economy of animalism among men, yet, to an extent that was never known before in the world, there is the spirit of sympathy of man with man disclosed. Never before has God been worshipped by the serving of his children as he is to-day. Never before was there such an adhesion as there is to-day to the words of Christ, "Inasmuch as ye do it unto one of the least of these, ye do it unto me." We worship a Christ that stands by the poor, by the slave, by the prisoner, and by the emigrant who lands, weary and discouraged, on our shores. We worship a Christ that identifies himself with the low and the needy and the suffering. We worship a Christ that is in the hospital among the sick. If worshipping God is worshipping Christ, I am Orthodox. I wish others were. I aver that Christ was never worshipped so much as he is to-day by the love, by the sympathy, and by the self-sacrificing helpfulness which we bestow upon all classes and conditions of men. Never before did the human race see a whole age and an organized nation putting their hands under the very bottom of society, and attempting to lift, not the crowned heads, not the middle classes, not the burghers and rich men, but mankind from the very lowest, taking the whole house up from its foundation. And while I see all reformatory societies attempting to reclaim men from intemperance, to cleanse our prisons, to purge out vice, to restrain all wrong; while I see the tendency everywhere to send, by showers of gold, the gospel to benighted nations, and to promote the mission cause at home, and to educate the slave and every living creature,— shall a man stand by and tell me that religion is going down? A religion that lets these alone is no religion; and a religion by which any man or community takes care of these, and in the love of God sympathizes with man, and cares for him,— that is the true religion.

When the potato was first sent to Ireland, they planted it, and did not know where to look for the fruit. And when it blossomed and bore its little seed-pods, they boiled these pods, and ate them, and did not like potatoes! If they had gone to the root of the matter, they would have liked them. And there are very many men who taste religion as it is shown in the pod, if I may so say; and they do not like this church, that doctrine, this ordinance, and that economy. What if you do not? These are not crops: they are merely the tools by which we try to raise crops. They are the machinery by which we work, and not the thing for which we are working. I never ate millstones; but I have eaten that which millstones have produced. And the things that grind out human love and kindness,— all may be defective; but the flour is the thing. And I say that never before was there so much holy flour ground as there is to-day.

There is one more thing that I think is true, and of which this celebration is significant; namely, that there is no statement of religion like religion itself. You cannot put into words the essential verities of religion. When you have used all the language that the vocabulary can give you, and tacked word to word, you cannot have made a belt that will go around the infinity and eternity of God. When by every figure that is known to fallible men, by all the sweetness of a mother's love, by all the purity of a child's love, by all the fervor of noble souls just mated, you have tried to represent God; when you have gathered up all things that are resplendent, and made them patterns of divine love,— you have done, as it were, nothing. The love of God that fills eternity, and that is marching down through eternities, bearing benison and benediction to countless spheres of existence, doubtless, besides our own,—when you attempt to put it into language and represent it by figures gathered by the limited experiences of men, it is as if you undertook to find timber for your navy in moss, and as if you undertook to decorate your cathedrals with the inconspicuous flowers and plants that grow too small but for the microscope. God is too big for language, too big for representation by human experience. The thing that most nearly represents God is a man that is living like God. And no man can draw that portrait or put it into language. We can see it, and we can rejoice in it; but, after all, the man that is like God is the best catechism and the best confession of faith. And we have learned one thing,—that, when we see such a man, he is God's, and he is ours. "All things are yours," says Paul. On that ground, I am as good a Catholic as there is in this world, except the pope and the cardinals and the bishops, and their doctrines. And from my ownership of every saintly woman and every saintly man no one can hinder me. They are mine, because they are God's; and I revere them and love them. There is a vast amount of true theology in the good living of the Catholic Church. There are men that rebuke our lukewarmness and our lives by the nobility of theirs,— multitudes of them; and they are all right. Whatever the church may be that makes them, theirs is the true theology. I go from that into the Episcopal Church. It is enough for me that she gave me my mother. Than that there can be no farther argument. The church that yields such blessings is not a church that I can contest, whatever her machinery may be. I ask: "What are the products? Where are the saints, men and women?" If they are Christ-like, they are all right. I go into the Unitarian Church. I want no better

Christians than I find there. They are orthodox, sound, by every Christian man and every Christian woman among them that makes piety beautiful in the eyes of mankind. I go into the Swedenborgian Church. Brother Ager is a good enough Christian for me. He is soundly orthodox, whatever he believes. No matter about that. I don't care what a man believes. What *is* he? That is my question. I say that what a man *is*, is his confession of faith. A man's life is more important than any statement of the philosophy of that life, or of the machinery by which that life was brought into existence.

It is true that some schools are better than other schools, that some methods of teaching are very likely to be better than some others, that some statements of doctrine are better than some other statements of doctrine in their aptitude to carry men on and upward. I will not discriminate as to which I think is the better, though I can well understand that there is a difference between one and another; but this I say, that when any man has been made a Christian, luminous of heaven, he does not belong to the church that bred him: he belongs to that universal church which has no exposition but in the sympathies of the universe; and he belongs to you and to me. And, sir, don't take on airs, as if Channing was your man. He is *my* man as much as he is yours. I have seen considerable of that spirit here to-night,— and I feel bound as a Christian to fight it,— as if you had a man that you would let us come and look at, as if we might be permitted to come on this platform and worship your hero. I thank God that you have some such men to worship and to present to us. It is a sign that there is a sort of grace with you. Your doctrines may be very imperfect; but, after all, there is a grace of God that goes with imperfection. All sorts of instruments have been employed in this world. Oftentimes, too, the instrument has been more than the prophet, as when Balaam went forth on his famous ride of old. And, since all sorts of instruments are employed by the good God, no matter what the instrument is, it is the man that is created.

Here was a man, in a dark day, in a day of controversy, in a day in which men stood very differently from the way in which they stand now; and I look upon the godly man and see a lambent flame of holiness. I see that he was a light kindled in a dark place; and the sweetness of his humility strikes me. He blushes in heaven to hear what is said of him on earth, if he attends to it,— though I think likely he does not. He was a good man. If he had been in the Roman Church, he would have been a saint; and he is not less a saint, because he was in the Unitarian Church. We have learned that man is a better exposition of Christianity than doctrines, or any of the various instruments of the church. We are learning to receive whom God receives; and whenever a man shows that he is acceptable to the Master, is wearing his spirit, and is blessed by his continual attendance, that man is sacred to us, no matter to what denomination he may belong. A man is more than doctrine, — and mankind are more than church and more than government. Next to God, the only valuable thing in this universe is living men; and all nature is prepared to take care of them. God is the Fountain and Cause of all things; and all nature and all time and all providence and all grace are so many ministering servants to develop manhood in men. And the only difference there can possibly be in our view of God is this: those views of God that tend to beat men down, and to beat down their moral sense, you may be sure are false views; while the views of God that tend to lift men up, to inspire them with a holy horror of sin, to lead them to aspire to holiness, and to give them a willingness to do kindness at their own expense, to live for mankind, and if need be to shed their blood,— such views are orthodox, however defective the system may be from which they spring.

When we look back, then, one hundred years, what do we see? The greatest change, I think, that has been produced in any hundred since the advent; and, when I look forward from this stand-point, it seems to me that we stand just about in the month of April in the history of the world as we do in this year. We have had our dead winter, we have had our blustering, controversial month of March, and now we have our month of April, which does not know exactly whether it has left March or whether it is entering into May; but it is on the way toward summer, and soon there will come the blossoms of May already anticipated; and after that will come June, the opal of the year; and then the summer; and then the harvest. We are on the full march; and, therefore, instead of looking back to the leeks and onions of orthodoxy in Egypt, the spirit of God, the spirit of philosophy, the spirit of wisdom, the spirit of true religion, is to forget the things that are behind, and to press forward toward the mark for the prize of our high calling in Christ Jesus.

Mr. Beecher resumed his seat amid the loud and long-continued applause of the audience, which had still remained unbroken, though it was now after eleven o'clock.

The following verses, from Bryant's "Thou hast put all things under His feet," were then sung by the assembly to the tune of "Coronation," as the closing hymn:—

> O North, with all thy vales of green!
> O South, with all thy palms!
> From peopled towns and fields between
> Uplift the voice of psalms.
> Raise, ancient East, the anthem high,
> And let the youthful West reply.

Lo! in the clouds of heaven appears
   God's well-belovèd Son;
He brings a train of brighter years;
   His kingdom is begun.
He comes, a guilty world to bless
   With mercy, truth, and righteousness.

O Father! haste the promised hour,
   When at His feet shall lie
All rule, authority, and power
   Beneath the ample sky;
When He shall reign from pole to pole,
   The Lord of every human soul!

The benediction was pronounced by the Rev. F. A. Farley, D.D., in these words: —

Now, with gratitude in our hearts, and thanksgiving and praise to God for this occasion, for all its sweet memories, and for all the blessed words it has caused to be spoken, may the grace of our Lord Jesus Christ, and the love of God, and the communion of the Holy Spirit, be with us, and remain with us always! *Amen.*

APPENDIX.

LETTERS FROM AMERICAN AND EUROPEAN FRIENDS.

Some of the following letters were read at the Memorial Meeting, as stated on a previous page. There was not time for them all. A few of the number were received shortly after the celebration was over, especially certain particularly interesting and valuable ones from abroad. They may not be omitted in this connection.

From Rev. GEORGE G. CHANNING.

MILTON, MASS., March 13, 1880.

My dear Sir, — I thank you for the cordial invitation to attend the celebration in Brooklyn of the one hundredth anniversary of my beloved brother's birth. I regret that my advanced age of ninety years will prevent my leaving home; but I shall be present in the spirit, though not in the body.

As I sit and muse on the other world, which is now in sight, — and for me death has not errors, — next to my Maker and my Saviour, do I think of him whose "Perfect Life" has given me so much joy. He was as revered in our early home as in the world. I only fear he has ascended too far for me to reach him.

With an old man's blessing on the occasion,

Faithfully yours,

GEORGE G. CHANNING.

From ELIZABETH P. CHANNING.

MILTON HILL, March 13, 1880.

Dear Mr. Putnam,— My father's failing sight, which is a great trial to him, precludes his putting more than his signature to his answer to your kind note.

His health is good, considering his great age. The deep religiousness of his family shines in him more and more. His communion with the other world is wonderfully clear and uplifting, and his childlike faith truly enviable. Hoping that the celebration will be all that you desire,

I am, sincerely yours,

ELIZABETH P. CHANNING.

From Rev. WILLIAM HENRY CHANNING.

HIGH STREET, BROOKLINE, MASS.

My dear Mr. Putnam,— Accept my very hearty thanks for your welcome to your admirably conceived Centenary Celebration, and to your pulpit.

It would give me the greatest pleasure to comply with your request, and to accept both invitations. But previous engagements, arranged for me by our friend Shippen, will make it entirely impossible either to preach for you on Sunday or to be with you during your meetings. If a free half-hour can be caught by the forelock, as it sweeps by, you shall have a brief note. But, really, you are so overflowing with rich contributions already that a word from me will seem like a meteor dropped on the sun when it is all ablaze with glory.

Let me, in a word, assure you that your plan for the Memorial Service is the very one that Channing himself would approve. If you ever see the *London Inquirer*, in the paper for March 20 you will find a letter from me, taking just the same view of the befitting mode of doing honor to a man whose self was forgotten in humanity.

Yours with cordial regard,

WILLIAM HENRY CHANNING.

From Rev. CHARLES T. BROOKS.

NEWPORT, April 1, 1880.

My dear Friend and Brother,— To you, and through you to all the members of the household of the faith who shall be gathered next week within your church walls, let me express the wish and prayer, on this auspicious opening day of April, the opening month of our centennial year, that the windows of heaven may be opened and pour down such a shower of blessings and graces that your hearts cannot hold them, and so will have to let the glistening streams gush forth to gladden and bless your neighbors and brethren around you.

Never did I so yearn to be in three, yea, four places at once as I shall on the approaching seventh of this month. I shall be there in spirit, if not simultaneously, yet in quick alternation of thought and sympathy.

God bless you and us all, and may this occasion be the means of drawing us nearer together and upward to the common home and onward in the common cause. Yours fraternally,

CHARLES T. BROOKS.

From MARY E. DEWEY.

SHEFFIELD, MASS., March 5, 1880.

My dear Sir,— My father finds it so painful an effort to use the pen that he desires me to write for him.

He thanks you for your kind and considerate letter, so kind and considerate that he is sorry for the answer he is obliged to make. On the twenty-eighth of this month, he will be eighty-six years old, and he is so weak that he cannot rise up or sit down or take a single step without help. Of course it is impossible for him to think of leaving home.

You give so pleasant an account of the persons you expect to see in Brooklyn on April 7th that he desires to send to them all his kind regards and friendly remembrance.

James Miller published, or rather republished, last winter, my father's Memorial Discourse on the Life and Writings of Channing, which he meant to be his last word concerning that remarkable person; and he does not feel able to add anything to it in the present condition of his health.

With his kind regards to you, I remain, dear sir,

Yours sincerely,

MARY E. DEWEY.

From Rev. SAMUEL OSGOOD, D.D., LL.D.

NEW YORK, April 7, 1880.

My dear Dr. Putnam,— The need of being careful of myself at this season, and Dr. Draper's grave caution, must keep me from your most worthy and winning festival to-day, which I was so eager to attend and to serve by my poor word.

Channing is a sainted name to me, and my early education was much under the influence of his mind. You may like to know that forty-four years ago, the first Sunday of April, 1836, I preached in his pulpit in his presence, received from his hands the Communion, and afterwards dined with him at his own house. He was very kind, spoke favorably of my attempt at a sermon on the Divine Light, and advised me always to state exactly what the subject was to be at the beginning.

I was at his funeral, October 7, 1842, and heard Dr. Gannett's noble sermon, and heard the cathedral bell toll.

The next year, May 24, 1843, I was married in front of that pulpit to my present wife, who was a lamb of the flock, who had been baptized by Dr. Channing himself.

I was brought up in the old Puritan church of Charlestown that was founded by John Winthrop, two hundred and fifty years ago, — where Dr. Jedediah Morse was pastor and where he opened the battery upon the Federal Street liberal preachers. My father, however, could not stand such rancor; and he was one of the leading seceders who founded the Unitarian Church in 1818, where James Walker and George E. Ellis were ministers. These are personal incidents that may not interest others; but they of course come to my mind at this time.

It gives me much grief not to be with you; but I am under orders from Dr. Draper, and after my speech of an hour and a quarter I must keep quiet. With the best wishes,

Fraternally yours,

SAMUEL OSGOOD.

From Mr. GEORGE RIPLEY.

661 FIFTH AVENUE, NEW YORK, April 4, 1880.

My dear Sir, — I greatly lament that the state of my health forbids my acceptance of your kind invitation for the 7th of April. In common with so great a company, both of the past and the present generation, who are indebted to Channing for the highest inspiration of their lives, and who revere his memory as the embodiment of purity and wisdom, of human virtue, and of Christian excellence, I would thankfully join in the tribute of affectionate veneration and admiring sympathy with which it is proposed to celebrate his birthday. As a young man, I looked up to Dr. Channing as a counsellor and guide; in more mature life, his friendship and sympathy were the brightest lights of my experience; since his death, not much less than half a century ago, I have found no more wholesome a study than the remembrance of his words and the contemplation of his character.

The germinal point of Dr. Channing's nature was reverence for man. Not a sentimental, effeminate love of humanity, which found vent in high sounding words, but a profound conviction that the divine attributes were truly manifested in human endowments. In his view, the presence of the Lord was not more conspicuous in burning bush or flaming mount than in the heart and conscience of man. To him, every human being was the true Shekinah which revealed the divine glory, and furnished a sacred altar for the worship of the Infinite and Invisible. Hence the ruling sentiment of his nature was reverence for humanity as the symbol of divinity. In this light, all earthly distinctions faded away. The dreams of ambition, the fashions of society, the fantasies of imagination vanished before the reason and *moral* nature which made man the image of God, the companion of angels, the heir of immortality.

Dr. Channing cherished an ardent faith in the progressive elevation of the human race, through the development of the affections, the intellect, and the ethical sentiments. Hence, he was always the strenuous champion of freedom of thought and action, limited by the sole condition of the supremacy of the higher powers over animal and selfish motives. He extended the hand of cordial fellowship to the thinker with his original thoughts, to the philosopher with his novel speculations, to the prophet with his celestial visions, and even sometimes perhaps to the enthusiast with his airy fancies and the dreamer with his idle dreams. But he rarely mistook the chaff for the wheat, the dross of the mine for the gold of the temple; and when his hand applied "judgment to the line and righteousness to the plummet," it was found convenient for shallow pretenders to hide their heads.

"Next to his love of humanity," if I may be allowed to repeat what I have elsewhere said, "Dr. Channing's most ardent passion was the love of truth, if indeed it was not his love of truth which inspired his profound devotion to the interests of humanity. He had no taste and little capacity for controversy. He delighted in the comparison of ideas, especially with men whose earnestness and good faith inspired him with confidence in their intentions; but the atmosphere of strife and debate was not congenial with his feelings, and prevented the free exercise of his highest faculties. He had no tincture of a dogmatic spirit. He was suspicious of broad generalizations, tracing their origin to imagination and eloquence more often than to accurate research, and hence was always disinclined to the adoption of a system. The tone of his mind was that of profound reverence. There was a solemn air in his manner, a tremulous urgency in his accents, when he spoke of 'the deep things of God,' of the mysterious greatness of the soul, of the divine capacities and destiny of man, which are sometimes faintly, but never fully reflected from his written page. Dr. Channing's mind attained its greatest freedom and power in his pulpit discourses. Neither in his colloquial intercourse nor in his familiar correspondence was he so free from formality, so natural and spontaneous, so entirely himself, as when addressing the congregation of worshippers on a congenial theme. His slight frame vibrated with emotion. His low voice, instinct with pathos and tenderness, touched the heart of every hearer. The scene was alive with more than dramatic intensity. It was not excitement, it was not enthusiasm, but the solemn communion of soul with soul."

With the hundredth anniversary of the birthday of Channing, what more significant wish can be expressed than that another century may witness the noonday brightness of the moral principles of which he rejoiced to see the empurpled dawn, and of which he was the illustrious harbinger and prophet!

I am, my dear sir,

Ever yours faithfully,

GEORGE RIPLEY.

From Rev. HENRY W. BELLOWS, D.D.

NEW YORK, April 6.

Dear Dr. Putnam,— It is a great disappointment to me to be necessarily absent from your Channing commemoration service in Brooklyn; and my only consolation is that I am kept away by the same motive that calls you together,—to bless and praise the name of Channing elsewhere, but in full sympathy with your grateful pæans. It is pleasant to know what a great company in Europe and America will be keeping this memorable centennial at the same hour, all bearing happy, hopeful testimony to the exalted worth and spiritual service, to the Church of the world, of the greatest religious light kindled by God's providence in this century. The growth and spread of Channing's hopeful views and consecrated spirit, so favorable to freedom, so fatal to priestcraft, so encouraging to spiritual liberty and yet so exacting of moral and spiritual fidelity; so high, yet so simple, and level to human wants; so rational, yet so profoundly based on faith; so unsuperstitious, yet so devout; so human, yet so divine; so appreciative of revelation, yet so just and honorable to human nature; so reverent of Christ and so respectful of humanity; so worshipful of God and so tender to his Fatherhood; so full of immortality, yet so appreciative of the significance, value, and happiness of the life that now is,— the growth and spread of these views, if not in the exact form he held them, yet in their essential temper and effects, fill me with joy and gratitude, and make the unsectarian celebration of his birth a hundred years ago, with such large consent and kind sympathy from many other Christian bodies, a most encouraging proof of the triumph of reason in religion, and of true religion in the region of the present and all the domain of man's life. May God and the spirit of Christ prevail in your celebration and over your hearts and minds! May he bless the pure and holy influence of the saint and hero of faith whom you celebrate, to his Church and to humanity! What could be better for God's kingdom than that Channing's disciples should multiply in all the churches of Jesus Christ?

Affectionately yours,
HENRY W. BELLOWS.

From Rev. JAMES MARTINEAU, D.D., LL.D.

5 GORDON STREET, LONDON W.C., March 26, 1880.

My dear Dr. Putnam,— Your letter, kindly welcoming me to your communion on the 7th of April, has, from accidental causes, reached me so late that it is doubtful whether the hurried words in which alone I can reply will reach you before that date. It would indeed be a true joy to me, could I personally join your thanksgivings to the Father of Spirits for the abode among us, for more than half a century, of one of the purest and loftiest of human souls. Where the tribute of love and reverence which one would render is so large and deep, it is impossible to throw it into a few defining sentences, which only fix what is forever flowing; it needs the swiftness of speech and the kindling of living sympathy to convey it in its intensity. If I already felt this in writing lately on the same subject to Mr. Schermerhorn, still more does a second experience bring my incompetency home to me. The impression left by Channing's life and writings is so simple in its greatness that, as with all things spiritual, its magnitude is rather in depth than in extent, and must rather speak for itself than be spoken of in verbal analysis.

But, on comparing his religious writings with those of the present day, I am struck with the fact that so small an element in them can be said to have lost its efficacy by the movements of justified opinion during the last forty years. Foreign reviewers reckoned it as a defect that he was no critic and no philosopher. And few scholars, I suppose, would now lay stress on his interpretation of texts or his mode of handling the Scriptures as historical and doctrinal sources. But how small a part do these superseded or questionable materials form of his grand scheme of thought and faith! With how slight a hand does he touch them! How little disposed is he to wield them with the air of external authority! They serve him chiefly as answering assurances of that inward witness, which is inseparable from the very essence of the soul, to its own greatness, its immortality, its kindred with the Infinitely Perfect, and as harmonizing well with that spiritual majesty in Christ which, in any case, is self-revealing. He escapes as fast as possible from the letter to the spirit, from the outward miracles to the personal holiness of the Son of Man, from the metaphysical distinctions to the "Moral Beauty of the Parent Mind." And so the natural gravitation of his thought carried it to the permanent ground of religion in the human mind; and the slightness of his critical and speculative culture saved him from alighting on any precarious resting-place, and delivered him freely over to the real experiences in which God and heaven will be forever found. And hence it is that his words still speak in sweet and solemn tones to a generation no longer at one with his historical theology.

Those whose Christianity carries in it a complex tissue of dogmas often look with a kind of wonder, not altogether respectful, at the simplicity of Channing's religion. They find it indistinguishable from morality; and no less a critic than Ernest Renan says that "his real mission was evidently altogether moral" (*Etudes d'Histoire Religieuse*, p. 380). If by the word "moral," he meant that which comes under the rule of right conduct between man and man in temporal society, the remark is not true. Channing had no hope of ever reforming conduct by mere criticism of its faults, or attention to men's relations.

"No particular vice," he said, "could be reformed alone." It is not by piecemeal pressure, such as law, interest, and opinion, can apply, that any higher moral level can be reached; but by a conversion which seizes the soul in all its dimensions at once, and lifts it into a transcendent relation to the Divine and Perfect Will. And the moment this relation is reached, we have emerged from the ethical sphere and passed into the religious. It is only, therefore, when we use the word "moral" to cover all that belongs to *perfection of character*, whether in relation to things human or divine (*i.e.*, only when we already embrace religion in it) that it can be applied as an epithet to Channing's "mission"; and then it ceases to *limit* that mission, and does but recite his own glorious doctrine: "Religion is moral resemblance to God."

His intense conviction that, except under true awakening of the conscience and the quickening of religious inspiration, moral reform was impossible, was just the feature which distinguished his hopes for the world from the dreams — which had fascinated him in his youth — of Rousseau, Godwin, Coleridge, and Southey, of a golden age of justice and equality and fraternity, secured by either revolutionizing the world or quitting its corruptions. These all depended on social construction, or reconstruction by men as they are; and, secured by only self-made bonds, might fall asunder as they had come together. But his reliance for the regeneration of the world was on the prior perfecting of the individual; on the inward spiritual rebirth of persons, taken one by one, merging the self-will of each in the All-righteous Will, dissolving spontaneously all false relations, and replacing low fears and passions by divine affections. In place of a public readjustment of rights, he looked for a private appropriation of duties. He could hope for this "kingdom of heaven," because there was no need for any new machinery or unheard of forces to bring it to pass. The power was ready,— hidden in every soul,— and needing only the sympathetic call from some faithful witness skilled to reach its slumbers and wake it into union with God. We want more of this noble faith of Channing's. It is itself a mighty agent in realizing its own predictions. Just as to credit another with goodness is often the way to make him good, so does moral hope for the world secure at least the first and hardest steps of the progress it contemplates. I know nothing more touching and more animating in any human life than the contrast between the pathetic tone of Channing's early ministry and the calm, unclouded joy of his last outlook upon the scene on which he left us. Surely it should rebuke and banish our poor despondencies. Believe me ever,

Yours very faithfully,

JAMES MARTINEAU.

From Rev. PHILLIPS BROOKS, D.D.

BOSTON, March 2, 1880.

My dear Dr. Putnam, — If it were possible, I would most gladly come and do honor to Dr. Channing. But I have engagements and duties here which I cannot escape, and which will make it quite impossible for me to be with you. I thank you truly for asking me, and am

Most sincerely yours,

PHILLIPS BROOKS.

From Rev. WILLIAM NEWELL, D.D.

CAMBRIDGE, March 29, 1880.

Dear Brother Putnam, — I felt greatly obliged to you for your kind invitation to attend the coming celebration at Brooklyn of Dr. Channing's birthday. For reasons already mentioned to you, I shall not be able to attend in person; and, as for special personal reminiscences, I do not think that I have any that will add novelty or interest to what will be said at that time and what has often been said or written by others. In fact, I had not much opportunity to know or to hear him. In my boyhood, and afterward, I attended with my father's family the New South; in College and at the Divinity School, the College Chapel. And, after my own settlement, of course I could hear him only on some week-day, at an ordination perhaps, or some special occasion. As he was settled before I was born, and I was not brought into personal relations with him in youth, and was separated from him in my Cambridge life, I had only a general acquaintance with him, as I suppose, with some accidental exception, was the case with the young ministers of my time. The delicacy of his health, his retired habits, his engrossment in the great subjects that occupied his mind, made him, latterly at least, somewhat of a recluse, and confined his society to a small circle of devoted admirers and friends, men and women.

Of the impression made upon me by his preaching, when I did hear him; of the effect produced by his voice, manner, look, and whole appearance in the pulpit, — I can only say what so many others have said before me. It was like the message of a sainted spirit speaking to us from the skies. It was perhaps in part the feeling of reverence and awe inspired by this, added to the other circumstances I have mentioned, which kept back many of his younger brethren from seeking a nearer acquaintance, and from what they imagined would be an intrusion on his studious privacy, an interruption of the precious time devoted to higher things.

Perhaps I may mention a single incident in which I was concerned that impressed me at the time, as illustrating casually his way of thinking and speaking. I had the opportunity in my early ministry of rendering important service to a young person in my parish, — an orphan of quick capacity and intelligence and good education, but without means, and amid unfavorable surroundings, from which I succeeded in extricating her, and putting her in the way of usefulness, self-support, and an honorable career, which her energy and good qualities enabled her to accomplish. Dr. Channing, through one of his parishioners, became acquainted with and interested in this matter; and, when I accidentally met him on the street in Boston one day, he stopped and had a few words with me about it, and, as he parted with me, said in his impressive way, "I think you have been the *instrument* of great good." He did not praise or compliment me, but looked upward, and would have me look upward, to the Higher Power, the Divine Providence, of which I was but the "*instrument*."

Though he did not mean what he said so naturally and simply as a lesson, I felt it as such, and was struck by it. You have asked me to write a hymn for the occasion, if I could not be present or do anything else. And this is the hardest of all to do, and I shrank at first from attempting it. But I felt bound by the call upon me at least to try, and, if perchance any inadequate contribution of this kind should answer the purpose, to send it for what it might be worth, a slight but well-meant token of love and reverence to be added to the birthday offering. Your suggestion of a hymn to the tune of "America" I put aside as out of the question, on account of the difficulties and restrictions of the verse which has so hampered S. F. Smith in his patriotic hymn. So I wrote a long-metre one, of which Channing was the subject throughout; but I did not altogether like it. Accordingly, I returned to your idea of "America," thinking that if I failed I should have ample excuse in the difficulties of the work, and that if I had any success it would be a pleasant victory over great obstacles. I thought too that it would be better for variety in the services to have it of a more general character, with the application *at the end* to Channing as the embodiment of the whole. I found it, as I expected, *very hard* to accomplish. And those who know and have had some experience of its difficulties will not wonder if I have failed to express *all* that they and I would have liked to have in it, and *as* we would have liked. The metre chains us down, and often rules out the best words. Silver and gold have I none, but such as I have I give. Ever yours.

WM. NEWELL.

From Rev. JOHN CORDNER, LL.D.

MONTREAL, April 4, 1880.

Dear Dr. Putnam,— I thank you for the invitation to your Channing celebration. It would give me great pleasure to be with you on that occasion, but I regret to say that this cannot be. We are to have a celebration of our own. Though absent in body, be assured I shall be present in spirit, and rejoice with you in every testimony borne to the honor, greatness, and ever-widening influence of our Saint, Prophet, and

Reformer. A holy man he was, clear in vision, faithful in his witness for the truth, and consistent in his application of the principles of righteousness to all the affairs of society. His simple eloquence, transparent in its sincerity, has commanded the attention of thoughtful minds in all parts of the civilized world to an extent beyond that of any other man of this century. His influence has been great in America, but I think it has been greater beyond the limits of America. Before I left the other side of the Atlantic, I had heard more of Channing as a name and a fame than I have heard on this side. And recent evidence makes it clear that his influence is still widening, not only in Europe, but in Asia. His influence on individual minds has been marvellous, lifting them into new spheres of thinking. "When I first came across Dr. Channing's writings," says George Hope, of Fenton Barns, "I was electrified by them. I felt he gave clear and articulate expression to the dim thoughts that had previously floated through my own mind. By his assistance, I looked higher up the blue vault above us, and obtained a clearer view of the Infinite Father." George Hope was a Scottish tenant farmer, and a very notable man, as Robert Collyer can tell you more at large. The service rendered by Channing to this man, dwelling in another hemisphere, has been repeated over and over again to hundreds of thousands of men and women in both hemispheres, in always increasing measure from year to year. The dawn of his influence rose in the first quarter of our century; and now in this, its last quarter, we see the light thereof steadily rising more and more unto the meridian of its perfect day. For this and for all it includes and signifies, let us be profoundly thankful. Ever yours faithfully,

J. CORDNER.

From Rev. F. H. HEDGE, D.D.

CAMBRIDGE, March 27.

My dear Dr. Putnam,— It would give me great pleasure to be with you in your celebration of the hundredth anniversary of Dr. Channing's birth into this human world, but various causes which I need not trouble you with prevent.

I send you herewith some words which I should be likely to have spoken, had I been one of the speakers on that occasion.

Sincerely yours,

F. H. HEDGE.

Dr. Channing has been called a reformer. I prefer to think of him as a prophet,— a prophet in the proper etymological sense of the word,— not a fore-seer, but a fore-sayer; an inspired asserter of truths, not new indeed, but which had never before found a condign organ and an adequate utterance. He was not a seer: he did not see farther than hundreds of his contemporaries; but what they saw with the eye of the understanding, he saw, so to speak, with the eye of the soul. I cannot claim for him the merit of originality. He cannot be said to have been in advance of the better thought of his time. His merit consisted in being the most *convinced* thinker, and therefore the most convincing exponent of that thought. Originality was not his gift, but effective utterance was. He was not a discoverer; but, as light existed before the sun, so truth floats vaguely in the mind of an age, and finds here and there a partial and imperfect utterance before the man arises whose office and privilege it is to concentrate the vague conceptions of his time, and to ray them forth in statements which carry warmth as well as light to all who have sense to see and hearts to feel. Such I conceive to have been Dr. Channing's ministry to his generation. He was the new-risen sun, the living word, of a better theology. And in due season his light "has gone out through all the earth, and his words to the end of the world."

Notably, he was not an iconoclast. He took no pleasure in demolishing. His sentiment was not destructive, but conservative. He turned gladly from that which needed to be overthrown, committing it to those who might be called to that work, and fixed his thoughts on that which needed to be affirmed and set up,— a reformer who put from him the implements of destruction, and wielded those of peace, as the prophets of old marched with the armed host to the land of promise, themselves unarmed.

In theology, he ranked as a Unitarian; but no man cared less for Unitarianism as the cause of a sect. He wished that pure and simple views of Christian truth might prevail in the world, but not that the Unitarian body might become dominant in the Church. He raised his voice against slavery, and labored in his own way in the cause of emancipation; but the abolitionists, as a political faction, could not claim him for their own.

He incurred the ill-will of some who could not make him a partisan; but he knew that it was not necessary to be popular in order to be useful, and the breath of man was not the inspiration that fanned his flame. He drew from imperishable sources, and therefore his work could not perish, nor his spirit wane. The forty years which have elapsed since his death have but added to its power. It might suit Mr. Cook and his employers, in view of the present celebration, to speak of "the diminishing influence of Channing." The wish in this case was father to the thought, or rather to the word. But all who are not blinded by sectarian bigotry must see that Channing's influence was never greater than now.

From Rev. E. TURLAND.

AINSWORTH, BOLTON, ENGLAND, Saturday, March 27, 1880.

Dear Sir,—It may seem strange to you to receive a letter from me, a perfect stranger; but I send you this line at the request of Mr. John Fretwell, of London, with whom you are well acquainted.

I have of late given some special attention to Scandinavian languages. The Rev. Brooke Herford first suggested to me to take up the study, and I have found great interest and pleasure in it. I receive the Swedish liberal Christian journal, the *Truth-seeker*, month by month; and I have written various brief articles on liberal religion in Scandinavian lands,— articles which have appeared in our English Unitarian journals, the *Christian Life* and the *Unitarian Herald*. A few weeks ago I had translated from the *Truth-seeker* a brief statement as to the translations of Channing's works (in whole or in part), which have been made into Icelandic, Swedish, Russian, French, Italian, etc.

Mr. Fretwell, seeing this, wrote to me, asking me to write to you, giving what information I can of efforts which have been made, or are being made, to make Channing's writings known in Sweden, Denmark, Norway, and Russia. He told me that, being unable to visit America to speak personally on "The Influence of Channing in Europe," he would write you a general survey of the whole field; but, thinking that I have special knowledge on the subject in relation to the northern countries of Europe, he would be glad if I would send you a few lines.

In my visit to the States in 1876, I was unfortunate from a Unitarian point of view. I was in time for the Centennial,—saw much of Philadelphia and the Exhibition, had a wonderful round trip (Pittsburgh, Chicago, Detroit, Niagara, Toronto, Montreal, Boston, Saratoga, New York); but I saw very few Unitarians and very little of Unitarianism. Most of the churches were closed, the ministers and many of the members being off for their holidays. Mr. Herford's church in Chicago was the only Unitarian Church in which I attended divine worship, though every Sunday I went to two services (on two Sundays I managed to attend three services) in churches of different denominations. I was not able to prolong my visit so as to attend the National Conference in Saratoga. Thus, from a Unitarian point of view, I missed very much. Generally speaking, it was a trip on which I shall look back with pleasure all the rest of my life.

Though I am thus unable to send you any special information as to the spread of Channing's influence in the north of Europe, I can express to you how thankful I am that you are celebrating Channing's centennial in such a noble and liberal manner. I can join with you in praising God for such a pure and saintly soul, such an apostle of Christ, such a prophet of God, as Channing proved himself to be; and I can send you my heartiest good wishes for the progress and general triumph in America of the cause of pure and undefiled religion, which you so ably and devotedly champion. It is Christ's own cause. It is the essence of good in all forms and faiths. Channing has done more for Unitarian Christianity than has been accomplished by any other single man. If we be faithful to his spirit, we shall do an increasing good; and there will be a time when it will be evident that Unitarians in America, England, and other lands, and liberal religionists in those and many other countries, have by no means labored in vain, but have on the other hand conferred upon the world a lasting and an eternal benefit.

As I say, I have written to you because Mr. Fretwell has asked me to do so. My letter, therefore, needs no apology. I send it to you as a sincere expression of good-will and heartiest good wishes.

Believe me to be, dear sir,
Yours very truly,
E. TURLAND.

From Rev. C. A. BARTOL, D.D.

BOSTON, March 8, 1880.

My dear Brother Putnam,— I have expressed my view of Channing in a paper to appear in a volume entitled "Principles and Portraits," in a few days. But I send greeting to you and your friends in the Brooklyn celebration. I trust that, with all the eulogy of the great Unitarian leader, there will be that discrimination of his qualities which is the best, and will prove to be the most lasting, praise. Channing made the chief protest of reason and conscience against superstition and what may be called the *immorality of religion* in our land; that is, a represented injustice in the divine temper and act. Human nature became in Channing's eyes a new Prometheus, crying out against the harsh Jove of the old theology. We are told, the office of the head is to lead the heart.

If so, it is yet the born servant of what it leads. Love alone can create the world, however Wisdom show the plan; and for the sentiment rather than the idea Channing stood. He was not a poet, a seer, a man of original suggestion or profound thought, characteristically reflective and contemplative as his genius was. His peculiarity was in the transcendent *justness* of his mind and moral sense, and in the unflinching courage with which he heeded the oracle within. He had no surpassing imagination; but there has not been a more rarely true *character* since the Master lived and spoke, all the simplicity of whose own manner this loyal and devoted disciple seems to have caught. Need it be said how, out of this same utter single-heartedness, came an eloquence among us which, in the style of calm and fervid conviction, has not been excelled? He had a sweet and lofty utterance all his own. The *cadence* of his period was an inflection, on which he ascended, and bore his hearers up. We do not stop with Channing; for we call no man lord. But we have had no one like him. His equals and in some ways superiors there may be, but not his peer. Of all I have walked and talked with in Boston streets, his figure in my memory stands how clearly apart. He was a lover of liberty, still more of truth and right. A retained advocate or special pleader he never was. He said only what was dear and precious to his own soul, and an idle or sophistical word could not leave his pen or his tongue.

Cordially to you all,

C. A. BARTOL.

From Rev. ROBERT SPEAR, England.

19 MORNINGTON ROAD, BOW ROAD, LONDON E.
24 March, 1880.

My dear Dr. Putnam. — It would certainly be a joy to me for ever if I could be with you at your celebration. This delight I cannot have, and so must wait for the happiness of meeting you and others in the grand assembly, if I should be worthy, where the blest presence of him we now honor may not only be felt, but seen. It may interest you to know that in the whole course of my experience I have never met with one person who has not confessed to the saved and saving influence of Channing's writings, and probably no Unitarian has had a larger correspondence with Unitarians of different countries than myself; and from every part of the compass the same testimony comes to me, from Iceland to India, and from Transylvania to the shores of the Pacific Ocean. In nearly every European language, parts — large parts — of his works are to be found. Among members and friends of nearly all the churches of the United Kingdom,— for I have correspondents in all,— the same testimony of light and sweetness is borne as among ourselves. I have just been reading how a grain of gold can be made to cover with its richness and by its ductility an immense surface; but this in no respects equals the wonder or the influence of that holy and beautiful soul whose memory we now try to honor. We are doing our best in England, in Ireland, and Scotland, to celebrate his centenary. I hear this news from every district, and do all I can to encourage and spread such a celebration.

It may interest your people to know that the shilling edition of Channing's Complete Works is the third on the list of the cheapest books of the world.—(1) The Bible, (2) Shilling Shakespeare, (3) Channing's Works,— and most sincerely I think this book will rank *third* in usefulness among mankind; and the best monument we can raise to Channing is the admiration of millions of souls for what they have felt in the study of his writings.

My love to all who honor Channing this day.

Yours very truly,
ROBERT SPEAR.

From Rev. THOMAS HILL, D.D., LL.D.

PORTLAND, MAINE, March 20, 1880.

My dear Dr. Putnam,— None know how much pleasure it would give me to be with you on the 7th proximo, but my engagements here will not suffer me to come until a week later, when I shall be in New York, and if possible call on you, and get direct from you some of the inspiration which you will draw from the occasion.

My personal indebtedness to the writings of Orville Dewey and Henry Ware, Jr., and to the living words of James Walker, was, in the days when my character was forming, far greater than to Dr. Channing, of whose writings I had read very little until within the last few years. I have come to him fresh, and without the distracting influence of early associations, and have found in him so much more of light, of sweetness, of strength, than I expected, that although, as I am fond of boasting, a Unitarian of the fourth generation, I have now for Channing all the enthusiasm of a new convert, and am doing what I can to circulate this spring in my neighborhood as many copies of his complete works as I can, and in whatever editions I can, from the English Centennial Edition upward. When I first came to New England, I heard Unitarian preaching characterized as "Channing and Water"; and I am sometimes fearful that in some vessels the mixture is altogether too watery, and would be greatly improved by the addition of more Channing. I am by no means an adherent of the view that he follows a leader most closely, who departs farthest from his line of thought. My favorite recreation is the mathematics, and they have taught me to regard true progress as consisting in the addition of truth to truth. What is once gained in them becomes a possession for ever; and I would regard the rejection of the positive truths which Channing held very much as I should regard the rejection of the propositions of Euclid or of Newton. Those great names have no authority to compel assent, but Channing's freedom, his intellectual power, his moral purity and elevation, his saintly fervor of piety, create a presumption of the truth of his views on the most vital theological questions, almost as great as that in favor of the soundness of Euclid's views on Elementary Geometry. May the anniversary meetings and action this spring have the effect not only of extending further his influence for liberty among those fettered and restrained by creeds, but of deepening his influence among us, leading us to more reverence, faith, and love, to a truer fellowship in Christ.

Ever truly yours,
THOMAS HILL.

From Bishop JOSEPH FERENCZ, Hungary.

Reverend dear Sir, — I was greatly interested to learn from the papers that our American brethren are to commemorate the centenary of the birth of Dr. W. E. Channing, in New York, on the 7th of April, in the same church which is at present under your ministerial care.

Great men, such as was Dr. Channing, do not belong to one nation or one country only, but to all mankind, because through their broad spirit they gained the right of citizenship in the heart of all peoples and all lands.

The great Dr. Channing especially deserved this right of universal citizenship, because he devoted his whole life to the promotion of the common interest of all mankind: namely, the cultivation of the soul and mind, and the spread of brotherly love.

He was a true disciple of Christ, and his spirit imbued his noble spirit.

We Hungarian Unitarians, too, belonging to a church which is in existence since three hundred years, profess Dr. Channing to be ours, and we are very proud indeed of having been able to publish five volumes, from his "Complete Works," in the Hungarian language.

But, beside the circulation of his useful and influential works, we desired to give a lasting expression of our honor and respect to him, by calling a professorship in our Divinity College after his name.

Allow me, dear sir, that on this account I may also express my most cordial greetings to you, in the name of the Hungarian Unitarians, on the occasion of the centennial anniversary of his birth.

You are celebrating now the centenary of the birth of one of your greatest men, just as we lately commemorated the tercentenary of the death of one of our great leaders. You had a Dr. Channing there beyond the Atlantic Ocean, and we had a Francis David here in the far eastern part of Europe. Both of them possessed an enlightened intellect and unprejudiced judgment, a noble heart and brotherly love, the freedom of conscience and of strong conviction; in a word, they were the great spiritual heroes of Christianity.

It seems as if the coincidence of these commemorations with each other would remind the American and Hungarian Unitarians of a closer union, as well as of the confirmation of our faith and hope in the future of Unitarianism.

Accept, reverend dear sir, once more, the expression of my sincere greetings; and at the same time I respectfully request you to convey it to the congregation of "the Church of the Saviour," and also to all the brethren present.

The grace and blessings of the only one God, the love of Jesus Christ, and the Holy Spirit which is shining forth from the works and lives of all great men, be and abide with you and with your churches and with us all for ever and ever.

Respectfully yours,

JOSEPH FERENCZ,
Bishop of the Unitarian Churches in Hungary.

KOLOZSVAR, March 26, 1880.

From Prof. DAVID SWING.

CHICAGO, March 31, 1880.

Dear Sir,— If the fame and virtue of Channing had not yet spread beyond the limits of that East where they began, I should accept your invitation, and journey all the way to your city, that I might feast upon his memory; but why should we Western men go toward you, when he whom we would recall has come to us?

In the war times, we learned that all souls of a certain divine quality "go marching on." This Channing spirit moves gracefully and peacefully across this great valley, and trails its rich garments along the aisles of even those churches where, could the eye see spiritual entities, it would discover the more severe shades of old European centuries; but it would mark that the nimbus around the Unitarian saint was at least as bright as that on the forehead of à Kempis.

Our city will hold in its largest hall a service in remembrance of a man of ideas and character so lofty. We dare not commemorate the heroes of war, and the worth of those who have been great in politics or literature or invention, and pass in silence the name of one who has led so many who have pondered over the problems of religion toward a Christianity of great truths and usefulness and overflowing with the spirit of Jesus Christ.

Your friend,
DAVID SWING.

From Rev. EDWIN M. STONE.

PROVIDENCE, April 3, 1880.

Dear Sir,— Your invitation to be present at the services in Brooklyn, on the 6th and 7th inst., in honor of the memory of William Ellery Channing, D.D., has been received. Nothing would afford me greater pleasure than in this way to show my respect for that distinguished man, and I deeply regret that pressing duties at home will preclude my participation in the enjoyments of that occasion. Your programme indicates that you have wisely decided that this anniversary is not to be confined within denominational lines. This seems to me to be in harmony with the spirit and well-known views of Dr. Channing; and it is eminently proper, on this centennial commemoration of his birth, that representatives of various religious bodies, appreciating the great thoughts with which his writings are now permeating America and Europe, should be invited to unite with you in exercises appropriate to the day. In my youth, it was my privilege to listen to the then two leading religious teachers in Boston, William Ellery Channing and Lyman Beecher. They represented two phases in theology, but, as it has ever appeared to me, the influence of each tending to the same end. Both were Christian reformers, unshackling the human mind and bringing it into harmony with the loving Father of all. While time endures, they will rank with the guiding minds of the Church of the living God.

With the prayer that this anniversary may serve to quicken activity in every cause advocated by Dr. Channing, and infuse a new vitality into the Church of Christ, to which he was faithfully devoted,

I remain fraternally yours,
EDWIN M. STONE.

From Rev. ANDREW CHALMERS, Cambridge, Eng.

4 BELVEDERE TERRACE, CAMBRIDGE, ENG., March 23, 1880.

Dear Dr. Putnam, — At the suggestion of my friend, Mr. Fretwell, I send you an assurance that the centenary of Dr. Channing will not be allowed to pass without due recognition in this ancient seat of English learning. The little band of Unitarians who have gathered round me here are familiar with the honored name and the imperishable thoughts of your saint and prophet; and, on their behalf, I heartily wish you a most successful celebration. Our numbers are but small; but we form a centre of cohesion, round which those may gather who have become imbued with the modern spirit, and yet retain their stability of faith. Our church is thus, if I may be pardoned the expression, a little like Dr. Channing himself, — a great soul in a somewhat small and fragile frame, — and perhaps, like him, it has appeared before the times were altogether ripe.

When lately in Transylvania, at the centenary of Francis David, I was struck by the frequency with which the beautiful name of Channing mingled in the rapid flow of Magyar oratory. It figured in the sermons and addresses with other great names round which the scattered sympathies of many nations gather, and at the festive assemblies it was greeted with enthusiastic cheers and the stirring music of the czimbalon. Since then, I have felt that Channing belongs not merely to the Western hemisphere, but to the whole wide world, and that his memory is inseparably allied with the promise of a better day for humanity. May the coming celebration be such as to show that, though truth be sown in weakness, it will be raised in power; and may this strengthen all who are fearlessly true to their best convictions and loftiest aims!

I am, dear sir,
Very faithfully yours,
ANDREW CHALMERS,
Minister of the Cambridge Free Christian Church.

From Rev. GEORGE H. EMERSON, D.D.

BOSTON, March 31, 1880.

My dear Friend, — Sincerely I thank you for the honor of an invitation to participate in the Channing centennial, and to enjoy your hospitalities on that very interesting occasion. Thirty years ago, I was more than a reader, something of a student, of Channing; and I have always held his memory in profound veneration. He helped me to attain a more philosophic and a more practical appreciation of Christianity. I could make heart and mind participate in the great ceremonial which will be more than a ceremony.

But duties at home, from which I cannot without extreme difficulty get release, will prevent my visiting Brooklyn the ensuing week. I must participate "in spirit." I cannot do so in person.

I need not hope that the occasion will be a very brilliant one; so much is evidently organized in advance. My heart's wishes go with it.

With thanks for your cordial invitation, which I reluctantly decline,

Fraternally,
GEORGE H. EMERSON.

From Rev. W. G. ELIOT, D.D.

WASHINGTON UNIVERSITY, ST. LOUIS, April 2, 1880.

Dear Dr. Putnam,— I shall be with you in spirit on the 7th, and in how many other places, with other groups of friends and brethren, to honor ourselves by the affectionate remembrance of that true advocate of the "liberty wherewith Christ hath set us free." William Ellery Channing. I write his name with pride and thankfulness that I knew and heard him in his best days, and can recall him now to my mind in the quiet dignity of manner that characterized him, expressive at once of gentleness and courage, but serving almost as a veil to his unsparing hostility to all wrong-doing, of whatever kind. Who would have thought, when seeing his mild, spiritual, self-hiding expression of face, or when hearing the subdued tones of his wonderfully sweet and flexible voice, that he could frown so sternly upon all falsehoods and shams, and inveigh with such aggressive vehemence against the oppressor, the bigot, the world-honored tyrants of the race? But in like manner was John, called the beloved disciple, also called Boanerges, the Son of Thunder. So true it is that TRUTH, deeply conceived and simply spoken, is the most potent spiritual force in building up the kingdom of righteousness and casting down the strongholds of sin.

Trusting that without anything of man-worship or blind discipleship we may enter into the spirit of his noble life, I join with you most heartily in your memorial service. We have an equally great work to do. The disturbing forces of society are as busily at work as ever. Slavery is dead, but the spirit of slave-holding still lives. The religious world has moved onward and upward both in faith and practice; but we are still, by many generations of growth, below the divine standard of Jesus Christ.

Let us thank God for the past, and take courage for the future, that we may quit ourselves like men.

Very sincerely yours,
W. G. ELIOT.

From Dr. FRANZ VON HOLTZENDORFF.

MUNICH, BAVARIA.

As the highest summits crowning a mountain-range must be seen from afar, to be valued in their orographical eminence, so religious and moral greatness will grow in the distance of times. The twentieth century is sure to arrive at a more perfect appreciation of what has been achieved by Channing than we now are enabled to attain to. The spirit of Channing is still wandering on his powerful pilgrimage throughout the world. His name is to preside over that œcumenical council of the Future, on which Christian life and morality shall be restored to original purity.

Dr. FRANZ VON HOLTZENDORFF,
Professor of Law, Munich, Bavaria.

From Prof. C. C. EVERETT, D.D.

HARVARD DIVINITY SCHOOL, CAMBRIDGE, MASS., April 4, 1880.

My dear Sir,— I regret that I am unable to accept your kind invitation to be present at the services to be held in Brooklyn on Tuesday and Wednesday next in memory of Dr. Channing.

We of the Divinity School have special reasons for gratitude and reverence toward him. His address at the dedication of Divinity Hall remains as a perpetual benediction; while the glowing words in which he drew the ideal of a large and free theological education laid down the principles which, we feel more and more, should underlie all work in this department of study, and made all who are interested in a ministerial training worthy of the age his debtors.

While I thus speak of his relation to the work which demands my special interest, and pay my special tribute to his memory, I know that this only illustrates the general nature of his influence upon the world. In every sphere of life, religious, social, and political, may be felt in like manner the helpful influence of his counsel and inspiration.

His work was manifold, yet in all its forms it had a single source in his faith in man and in the divine life to which he is called.

Yours very truly,
C. C. EVERETT.

From the DUTCH PROTESTANT ASSOCIATION, Holland.

TO THE UNITARIANS PREPARING TO CELEBRATE THE CENTENARY OF CHANNING'S BIRTH:

Dear Brethren,—We beg to address you a few simple words on the day on which a century ago William Ellery Channing was born. If it is your duty and your honor to commemorate the birth of that great and good man, who indeed was yours from the beginning to the end of his glorious career, we feel as if our native country had some right to be represented at your celebration. Holland was among the first of the nations of the European continent to acknowledge Dr. Channing's merits and to translate many of his immortal words into its own language. But it is not a right that we claim: it is rather a deeply felt duty which we perform in paying a small tribute of gratitude to his revered memory. If there are among us those who from the bondage of the letter have passed to the liberty of the spirit, whose Christianity stands high above the division of creeds, who value Christian character and life far more than any formula, we owe that, at least in part, to Dr. Channing's influence. A Christian prophet and a Protestant saint! In bestowing these names upon your great countryman, the Dutch not only echo what has been said by others, but at the same time give expression to what they have experienced themselves in listening to his mighty voice and looking upon his lofty example.

"The Nederlandsche Protestantenbond" (Dutch Protestant Association), of which we are the representatives, has no special commission to speak in the name of all those who in this country have profited by Dr. Channing's teaching, and cherish his memory. If circumstances had allowed it, many would have joined us in this act of respectful sympathy, who do not belong to our Society. Though not possessing any definite theology, our Association, if judged by the majority of its members, does not hold and propagate that form of Christian doctrine which Dr. Channing taught his contemporaries. Nevertheless, we claim our humble place among those who follow in his footsteps and who continue his work. Our aim, as expressed in our Statutes, " the free development of religious life within the churches and without their boundaries," was eminently his during his whole lifetime. That aim is yours too. And therefore we feel very confident that you will not forbid us to participate mentally in your commemoration, which, without ceasing to be national and Unitarian, from the nature of its object assumes an international and universal character, in accordance with the spirit of broad catholicity, of which Channing was the apostle. May

God prosper your endeavors to spread Christianity, not as a system, but as a principle of true religious and moral life! Channing's name is the honor of American Unitarianism. May it never lose sight of the great responsibility which that name lays upon all those who glory in it!

On behalf of the Dutch Protestant Association (de Nederlandsche Protestantenbond).
VAN BONEVALFAUSE,
President, Professor at Law, University Leyden.
J. VAN LOENEN MARTINET,
Secretary of the Reformed Church, 2 Walle.
LEIDEN, 2 Walle, 20 March, 1880.

From Rev. C. C. SEWALL.

MEDFIELD, Feb. 11, 1880.

My dear Sir,— I heartily thank you for the invitation to attend the celebration of Dr. Channing's birthday, and to offer such reminiscences as I may retain of him there. It was never my privilege to be personally acquainted with that great and good man, and the few reminiscences of him which I could offer would not be worthy the occasion. Excepting those of a few instances in my early life, there are none other than are common, I presume, to all who knew of his life and ministry. In my boyhood, it was required of me to commit to memory a hymn on Sunday, to be repeated at the close of the day to my parents or some member of their family. I well remember how, on one of these times, my sister read to me Channing's "Sermon to Children," and that I was so affected by it as to beg that it might be read to me again and again, at other times. Nor was the impression I received from it ever effaced from my mind. It somehow brought him very tenderly and closely to my heart, and was the cause of the interest which I felt ever afterwards in him and in all that I heard and read of him. After completing my preparation for college at Exeter Academy, I was obliged to go to New York and reside with my brother,— a merchant there,— and as a clerk in his counting-room. I there heard Dr. Channing's first sermon to the Unitarians in New York, which he read to them in the parlor of Mr. Russell's house. I remember the satisfaction and delight expressed by the friends who were present. I think it strengthened and quickened the impulse already felt to establish a Unitarian Society in the city. Dr. Channing was then on his way to attend the ordination of Mr. Sparks at Baltimore. On the Sunday following (I think it was), public religious worship was held by the Unitarians in a hall of the Medical

College. I remember the presence of several of the delegates to the ordination at Baltimore, and of an audience nearly filling the hall. Not long afterwards a room was procured and fitted for the purpose of public worship, in a building on the corner of Broadway and Reade Street, where the Unitarians worshipped, I think, until their church was built. During this interval, I left New York, and became a school-teacher in Roxbury, in Dr. Porter's parish. I then walked into Boston occasionally to hear Dr. Channing preach. The tones of his voice and power of his words never failed to touch and move my heart. I was present at the funeral of one of his parishioners,—my cousin, John Gallison, Esq.,—when his emotions were so tender and affecting as to prevent his utterance and move him to tears; and fresh and deep impressions of his peculiar excellence in the offices of the ministry were left upon my mind. He who was so moved himself could not fail to move others. After this, I have no particular reminiscence of Dr. Channing, and none other than would be common to all who knew of his life and ministry. I may say, however, that I well remember it was the influence of his publications which gave birth to a Unitarian Society formed in Bowdoin College—then an exclusively Orthodox institution—while I was there. A few of my fellow-students met, and formed this society for the purpose of procuring a library and of circulating Unitarian publications. A library was obtained, and by an article of the constitution was to be merged in the college library, if the society should be dissolved or become extinct. I am the only one living of the original founders of the society, and do not know what has been the fate of it. Our friends, Dr. Peabody and Mr. Pike, were, I believe, members while they were in the college. And I am sure the moving impulse to its formation was the influence of Dr. Channing's writings upon our minds.

Believe me, dear sir,
Very truly your friend,
C. C. SEWALL.

From Hon. S. E. SEWALL.

BOSTON, April 4, 1880.

My dear Sir,— Your invitation to me to be present and speak at the celebration of Dr. Channing's birthday is before me. I regret that I cannot be at Brooklyn on so interesting an occasion. But as I was personally acquainted with him, and often heard him preach, I will try to give some idea of the impression he made on me and others.

He was a slender man, not above the middle height, apparently in poor health, but with expressive eyes, black hair, and a face stamped with intellect and sympathy. In the pulpit, he used no obvious arts of oratory; but his voice was clear, sweet, and full of feeling, so that, with very little gesture, every word he said struck a responsive chord in the hearts of his hearers. I shall say nothing of the style or substance of his discourses or writings, which I am sure will be better described by others than I could do. I will only add that those who listened to him, as they left his church, felt a moral elevation which they were sure would affect their future lives, a sentiment often expressed by them. His reading of the Bible and hymns refixed the attention of his audience. There was no effort in it. But the tone and emphasis were so true to the thought and feeling of what he read, that he often seemed to bring out a meaning in the words that had escaped us before.

His eloquence and weight of character rendered him a great power in the anti-slavery movement. At its very outset, he spoke with perfect freedom against slavery from his pulpit to a congregation many and probably most of whom did not sympathize with him. During the rest of his life, his thoughts dwelt much on the subject, and he spoke, wrote, and published abundantly upon it. I well remember a sermon which he preached in his own church, in which he said emphatically: "Man cannot have property in man." A very respectable lawyer, on our leaving the church, at this time said to me: "I do not know what Dr. Channing meant. Slavery is legal in all the Southern States."

One or two circumstances, though very fully related in Dr. Channing's Life, by his nephew, are so imprinted on my recollection that I venture to refer to them briefly. When Elijah P. Lovejoy was murdered at Alton, Ill., for attacking slavery in his paper, Dr. Channing proposed that a meeting should be held in Faneuil Hall to express the sentiment of Boston on this crime against the freedom of the press. A petition was accordingly prepared, headed with his name, asking the Mayor and Aldermen to grant the use of the hall for this purpose. A counter petition was immediately sent in to them; and they, yielding to the pressure of what seemed to them public opinion, refused the hall. Without delay or hesitation, Dr. Channing published an address to the citizens of Boston, in the *Daily Advertiser*, vindicating his course and appealing from this decision. This appeal was seconded by a meeting in the Court House. A new petition for the hall, again headed by Dr. Channing, was granted, and a great meeting held there. Dr. Channing was the first speaker; others followed; and resolutions drawn by Dr. Channing were adopted.

It was at this meeting that Wendell Phillips first surprised and charmed his hearers by his eloquence, and established his reputation as a great orator. I make no comment on Dr. Channing's course on this occasion. The bare statement of the facts is the highest eulogy.

One other recollection comes to me illustrating Dr. Channing's character. Abner Kneeland was indicted for blasphemy for an article in a newspaper published by him. He was convicted, and sentenced to three months' imprisonment. A petition for his pardon was at once drawn up with Dr. Channing's concurrence and aid, his name being first of the signers. The petition failed in its direct object, but there have been no prosecutions for blasphemy since Abner Kneeland's.

Yours truly,
S. E. SEWALL.

From Rev. G. W. HOSMER, D.D.

SALEM, March 20, 1880.

Dear Dr. Putnam,— I thank you for your kind invitation to Brooklyn, to have part in the solemn joy and quickening inspiration of centenary thoughts and memories of our great prophet-brother, Dr. Channing. What an inheritance we have had and still have from him,— what riches of thought, sentiment, character! Would that we might make the most of it all for ourselves and for the world, for now and for all time. We are trustees. Alas for us, if we fail to make the most of these spiritual riches!

The appreciation of Dr. Channing, and the great reception of his influence in Europe and throughout the world, is an encouragement to us to do more and more to make him known.

I should be glad to be with you at Brooklyn on the 7th of April, but I have promised to be at Newport. May joy and peace be with you!

Very cordially,
G. W. HOSMER.

From Rev. JOHN COTTON SMITH, D.D.

NEW YORK, ASCENSION RECTORY, April 7, 1880.

My dear Dr. Putnam,— I am prevented at the last moment from attending the meeting in commemoration of Dr. Channing, at which you kindly invited me to speak. I regret this, because I should have valued the opportunity to express my sense of the indebtedness of the world to Dr. Channing for a powerful influence in behalf of some of the most important principles of Christianity.

Such an influence he exerted in behalf of the principle that true Christianity and philanthropy are inseparable. He taught men that the service of Christ demands unceasing warfare against every form of evil by which humanity is oppressed. His intense earnestness and clear moral and intellectual convictions gave immense power to his assaults upon slavery, war, intemperance, and social selfishness. Other men have taught the same truth; but Dr. Channing taught it when it seemed to have been forgotten, and when its practical application roused the most bitter hostility even among good men.

Another most important principle which owes a great deal to Dr. Channing is this: that the truths of the Christian religion are and must be in harmony with reason and the moral sense. It is difficult now to form any adequate idea of the extent to which the New England theology at one period represented God as anything but reasonable and good. The men who dissipated this delusion, and taught that the ultimate standard of our conception of and feelings toward God must be found in reason and the moral sense, rendered an invaluable service to the world. Among these men, Channing was in his day perhaps the most eminent.

For these reasons, though differing widely from him in his view of the person and the work of Christ and the nature of the Christian Church, I honor and revere his memory. I find myself drawn very close in spirit to a man who could say, as Channing does of Christianity: "Its great lesson is self-sacrifice. Its distinguishing spirit is divine philanthropy suffering on the cross. The cross, the cross,— this is the badge and standard of our religion. I honor all who bear it. I look with scorn upon the selfish greatness of the world, and with pity upon the most gifted and prosperous in the struggle for office and power; but I look with reverence on the obscurest man who suffers for the right, who is true to a good but persecuted cause."

I have written these few words in regard to Dr. Channing at your request, and beg you to believe me,

Faithfully yours,

JOHN COTTON SMITH.

From Rev. JOHN H. MORISON, D.D.

BOSTON, April 5, 1880.

Dear Dr. Putnam,— A slight illness, which I have got over, leaves me too weak to venture to be with you this week. It is a great disappointment to me.

Apart from his genius, the one thing that gave Channing his power was his perfect truthfulness. His convictions were a part of himself. His words came instinct with life because they *were* his life. What he spake, that he was. He did not talk about principles; but the principles themselves came living from his lips.

Wishing you all success in your celebration,

I am most truly yours,

JOHN H. MORISON.

LETTER FROM UNITARIANS OF HUNGARY.

(Translated by Miss Mary Lyman.)

To the Pious Believers of the Unitarian Church in Brooklyn:—

Salvation and all good, from the one true God!

We have received the information through the newspapers, and through our dear brother in the faith, John Fretwell, the zealous friend of our schools, that you were making preparations to celebrate the hundredth anniversary of the birth of Channing, the wisest teacher of humanitarian Christianity in this century. The sympathetic attention of the world therefore rests upon you. It is an undertaking worthy of the free people of North America, a fitting tribute to the great man, and well-pleasing to God. We bow before your greatness of heart, and implore God's blessing on your noble effort. Many thousand Hungarians do this with us. We wish that your project may have brilliant success, and that your holy work may leave behind traces rich in blessing in the life of Christianity.

The recently formed First Hungarian Unitarian Filial Church congregation of Budapest will, as soon as it has obtained the consent of the highest church council, send you and the Unitarian Churches of North America and England an address, in order to give you therein an explanation as to our affairs and efforts, and in fitting manner to ask for your sympathy and brotherly assistance. In the mean time, we obey the impulse of our heart on the occasion of this festival, which has especial interest for us as a new church congregation, and greet you through these lines with the genuine warmth of Christian love and with the brotherly affection of a kindred faith.

William Ellery Channing is your countryman; but his soul, aflame with Christian love, is known to us also. To you belongs only his name; his spirit belongs, in its universal working, to all humanity. We have also translated his works, and published them by the aid of our North American brothers in the faith. The same are already read in Hungary to-day by thousands in private, as well as in the reading-rooms of the public libraries and universities of the Hungarian youth. The ideas unfolded in them are disseminated in the collected Confessions of Faith belonging to these institutions. The literary circles of Hungary have expressed themselves in the most appreciative manner with regard to the author of these works; and, even in years just elapsed, prominent men of learning and of high social position have gone over to us, and such conversions take place frequently, even now. All this may be ascribed, in a high degree, to the influence and winning power of Channing's Works, and to the free spirit and stand-point of faith of the English-American Unitarians.

These ideas have, among us, fallen upon a well-prepared, deep, and fruitful soil. It is already three hundred years since the Unitarian confession of faith has received legal sanction and equal authority with the opposing creeds in the Siebenburg parts of Hungary, and a well-organized central church government in one of the most cultivated cities in the land, Klausenburg, and numbers in addition thereto the factors and standard-bearers of political freedom and universal culture. The first founder and bishop of our church — who also enjoyed in his time a European reputation, whose three hundredth anniversary we celebrated last year, and whose life, career, and glorious battles for the establishing of the faith, one of the ablest of our fellow-believers, Alexius Jacob, has described — died as a martyr to that teaching whose acceptance your fortunate countryman and apostle of the faith, Channing, so gloriously achieved in this century by the subtlest human thinking.

Honored brothers in the faith, we beg you earnestly to turn your attention to this circumstance: The successful dissemination of Channing's religious ideas opens in our fatherland a wide field, and throughout the south-eastern countries of Europe, those lying on the Danube and even down into Turkey, where Hungary is especially called upon to transplant Western culture. Many Hungarians, also, are to-day living in Constantinople, who have there scientific and literary associations, and who are in constant intercourse with their Hungarian homes. Recently, Gabriel Bálinth has gone there,— a Hungarian scholar, tutor in the Budapest University, a Roman Catholic who became converted to the Unitarian faith, and, commissioned and partly assisted by the Hungarian Academy of Sciences, travelled in the East for several years, and who has now received the appointment to an influential position in the Finance Bureau of Bagdad.

Our English and North American companions in the faith could accomplish successful missionary work in Hungary, and, through Hungary, in the East. Their sacrifices would bear here a rich harvest in the spread of Unitarian Christianity, and of Western, especially English, civilization.

We commend you to the protection of God, and our interests to your hearty sympathy, and remain, with respect and brotherly greetings in the faith, at Budapest, the capital of Hungary, March 20, 1880, your loving brothers, and companions in the faith, in Christ.

(Signed by)

PRINCE ARTHUR ODESCALCHI,
Of Szarém.

Dr. PETER HATALA,
Public and Professor in Ordinary at the Royal Hungarian University in Budapest.

BLASIUS BARON ORBAN,
Member of the Chamber of Deputies in Hungary.

ALEXIUS JAKOB, M.P.R.,
Member of the Hungarian Academy of Savants.

ARON BUZOGANY,
Secretary of the Department of Education and Public Instruction; Secretary of the Unitarian Filial Church Congregation in Budapest.

THE INFLUENCE OF CHANNING'S WRITINGS IN EUROPE.

By JOHN FRETWELL.

LONDON, March 20, 1880.

(1.) *My dear Dr. Putnam,*—Your invitation to address the meeting at Brooklyn on Channing's influence in Europe recalls to me so many inspiring memories that I would gladly cross the Atlantic to be with you on this grand occasion, and listen, as I have often listened in former days with charmed ear, to the eloquence of the speakers who are to address our people in praise of William Ellery Channing.

But I have to speak in Germany on that very day; and, on the whole, I shall be better occupied in trying to spread the influence of Channing in the Old World than in talking about him to those who know his work better than I on the Western Continent.

I gladly accede, however, to your request that I would send you a letter containing some account of the influence exercised by the works of your great countryman, here and on the continent of Europe. While, to procure you still more detailed information, I have asked competent persons in every European country to send you direct reports on the influence exercised by Channing on their respective peoples.

I. GREAT BRITAIN.

(2.) Here the testimonies are so numerous that my only difficulty is to select a few, while I must necessarily omit a large number of almost equal value. The great Christian philosopher who has contributed most in our time to the development of Unitarian Christianity, Professor James Martineau, has frequently paid tribute to his American forerunner; and I will quote only one expression from his discourse preached before the British and Foreign Unitarian Association, May 19, 1869, wherein, after speaking of the *Religion of Causation*, as taught by Priestley, he goes on to Channing's *Religion of Conscience*, and says: —

"When the tones of the New England prophet reached our ears, why did they so stir our hearts? They brought a new language, they burst into a forgotten chamber of the soul, they recalled natural faiths which had been struck down, they touched the springs of a sleeping enthusiasm, and carried us forward from the outer temple of devout science to the inner shrine of self-denying duty. The very inspiration of the new gospel, in what thought does it lie? The greatness of human capacity for voluntary righteousness, for victory over temptation, for resemblance to God."

(3.) When we listened at Unity Church to these words of James Martineau, we had among us one whom we loved to call the English Channing, Martineau's colleague and friend,— John James Tayler, the Principal of our Divinity School.

Saintly as Channing, he had a wide and thorough knowledge of the tendencies of modern speculative thought and the results of modern Biblical criticism. In that most fascinating of all ecclesiastical histories, his *Retrospect of Religious Life in England* he defends Channing against the reproach of having written no great work, saying of Channing's publications: —

"Addressed to present feelings and interests, and eagerly absorbed by them, they only infused the principles of which they were the vehicle more deeply into the heart of society. Such has ever been the literary character of men who have acted most powerfully on the general mind of their time. It was that of Wesley; to a large extent, it was that of Baxter and Luther. His function was rather that of the prophet than of the scholar or philosopher."

And again (p. 306, edition of 1876): —

"The earnest and devotional character of his mind was altogether averse to the wild and gratuitous scepticism which has infected so much of the theology of the Germans. He does not appear to have drawn in any instance direct from German stores of erudition and philosophy. Yet his writings — perhaps in America, certainly among the Unitarians of England — have contributed to prepare the public mind for more truly estimating the scholarship and comprehending the intellect of Germany, and furnished a medium of transition from the school of Priestley, which, on nearly every point, is at war with them."

II. IRELAND.

(4.) Turning from England to the sister isle, we find there, in the excellent little book of Rev. John Orr, of Comber, a clear and succinct statement of the services rendered by Channing and his school in "modifying the dominant theology, reconciling the sceptic with religion, and promoting every good form of humanitarian enterprise"; fully indorsing the language used by Starr King, when he calls the "single contribution of Channing's thought and character to the influences that mould our civilization equivalent in value almost to the collective achievements of whole churches."

III. SCOTLAND.

(5.) Having quoted from the printed utterances of three representative theologians, let us now turn to a Scotch farmer, "George Hope, of Fenton Barns." This gentleman was a man of no small influence in Scotland. His essay on the repeal of the Corn Laws was one of the three which were selected as worthy of a prize and of publication, the other two prize essayists being also Unitarians, — Mr. Arthur Morse and the afterwards so celebrated William Rathbone Greg. When the three great "Corn-leaguers"— Cobden, Bright, and Ashworth — went to Scotland to speak in favor of repeal, one of them asked to what religious denomination Hope belonged, and, on hearing that he also was a Unitarian, expressed his surprise that these men *with no religion* should be such philanthropists!

Let us see to whom he owed the inspiration of philanthropy. In a letter addressed to his brother in Canada, he writes: —

"When I first came across Dr. Channing's writings, I was electrified by them. I felt that he gave a clear and articulate expression to the dim thoughts that had previously floated through my own mind. By his assistance, I looked higher up to the blue vault above us, and obtained a clearer view of the Infinite Father. But it is not alone in religious sentiment, exactly so called, that I have been educated by his instructions. From him I have obtained juster views of the rights and worth of the human race. Who that reads his writings can be insensible to the sin and misery of war, to the great curse of slavery, to the guilt of ambition, which makes murder the trade of thousands, subjugating men's souls, and breaking them to servility as the chief duty of life?"

The man who thus escaped by Channing's aid from the gloomy bondage of Calvinism laid twenty years later the foundation-stone of the Second Unitarian Church in Glasgow. His farm at Fenton Barns became renowned through all England, not merely because from poor beginnings he raised it to a model of successful farming, but also on account of his admirable treatment of his laborers.

IV. CHANNING PROPAGANDISM IN BRITAIN.

(6.) The case of George Hope is but one among hundreds of instances of the robust virtue inspired among our people by the direct or indirect influence of Channing's word; and it is not to be wondered at that numbers of our preachers, from Robert Aspland down to John Page Hopps, have used every available opportunity of popularizing his thought, and of bringing his works within the reach of all who were open to their influence. A cheap edition was published by Rev. Mr. Maclellan, of Belfast, in Northern Ireland. Joseph Barker, a preacher of the Methodist New Connection, recommended in his periodical, the *Evangelical Reformer*, the perusal of Channing's works; and after his expulsion, on the ground of heresy, from this Connection, he published, with the aid of money furnished by a Unitarian family in Leeds, a cheap edition of Channing's Works, bringing them within the reach of thousands, who but for him would probably never have seen them. The British and Foreign Unitarian Association has always distributed large quantities of Channing's separate discourses, and, during the secretaryship of the Rev. Robert Spears, sold and gave away twenty-four thousand copies of the complete works, distributing them not in Britain alone, but among readers of English on the continent, in India, and our colonies.

Since his withdrawal from the secretaryship of the Association, Mr. Spears has established a missionary paper, *The Christian Life*, *a Unitarian Journal*, which distinguishes itself from other papers in our denomination by its making the promulgation of those views taught by Channing its special object. This journal contains also the richest fund of information about the spread of Channing's influence throughout the world, while its zealous editor is now working hard to celebrate the one hundredth anniversary of Channing's birthday by circulating one hundred thousand copies of the complete works, including the "Perfect Life," at the price of twenty-five cents.

V. Channing's Influence in the Orthodox Churches of Britain.

I. Sam. ii., 36: "And it shall come to pass that every one that is left in thine house shall come and crouch to him for a piece of silver and a morsel of bread, saying, Put me, I pray thee, into one of the priest's offices, that I may eat a piece of bread."

(7.) The prophecy of the man of God to Eli is applicable to so many ministers of the State Church and of the popular theology that it is very difficult to obtain clear statements of the impression made by Channing upon conformists.

The English abolitionists and the leaders of our Peace Society, like Henry Richards, M.P., have of course recognized the immense services done by Channing to their cause.

The Rev. J. Baldwin Brown, most eloquent and enlightened of the Congregationalists, and Thomas Hughes, M.P., Q.C., the pupil of and biographer of the good and great Dr. Arnold of Rugby, shew their admiration of Channing by taking part in our London commemoration.

Other ministers, of kindred spirit to Channing's, like F. W. Robert, son of Brighton, Stopford Brooke of London, and the Rev. F. D. Maurice (himself the son of a Unitarian), have, while bold enough in expressing their sympathy with Channing, probably injured thereby their prospects of advancement; and many who, like Canon Farrar, approach the direction of his teachings on the subject of eternal punishment, ignore him altogether.

In his Bampton lectures on the "Divinity of Jesus Christ," Canon Liddon has made frequent quotations from Dr. Channing, for the purpose of attempting their refutation; and he even uses the brilliant but untenable arguments of Renan in the attempt to show that Channing, if he had lived to-day, would have been either a Trinitarian Christian or not a Christian at all. Arthur Penrhyn Stanley, the Dean of Westminster, who refused a bishopric, preferring the office of chaplain in ordinary and confidential adviser to our Queen, who has always shown himself brave toward the bishops, though sometimes too deferent to court influence, who called our Priestley "the last of the pilgrim fathers," has several times expressed his admiration of the work done by Dr. Channing.

How many laymen and preachers have been won over to our ranks by the perusal of Channing's works, it is hard for me to say; but I know the number to be large, and to his writings, more than to those of any other Unitarian, may be applied those words of James Freeman Clarke:—

> "Those men we honor here,
> Sent to bring back the gospel's blessed youth,—
> Who knew no doubt, no fear,
> And so renewed man's faith in God and truth:
> Far as thought goes, their influence has gone,
> Through iron gates and walls of stone
> Built around churches to keep out all change
> By magnetism strange.
> Their simple, honest word has entered in
> Unchallenged, passed all creeds;
> And now their thought,
> Which fifty years ago seemed rankest sin,
> Is freely welcomed and around us taught."

VI. THE GREATEST TRIBUTE OF ALL.

(8.) There was one man in Europe who had more capacity to judge of Channing's true place among the prophets of God in history than almost any other, English or German, theologian or statesman. This was C. Josias von Bunsen. Sent by the King of Prussia in 1834 to Rome, to arrange the differences between the Prussian government and the Pope, and in 1841 to England, to arrange with our government for the establishment of a Protestant Bishopric at Jerusalem, he became the friend of our Queen, of Prince Albert, and of Dean Stanley. Devoted to the very close of his life to the study of the Bible, he was at once a statesman, a scholar, and a liberal though always a Trinitarian theologian; and, striving to enrich English theology, on the one hand, with the results of German scholarship and philosophy, he took to the German Church, on the other, his observations of the practical methods of Christian work, which are peculiar to the voluntary church organizations in England and America.

The unprejudiced opinion of such a man is of more value than that of any one belonging to our own body, however great he may be.

And what does Bunsen say? (See his *God in History*, Book V., p. 268):—

"Now since Channing spent his life in indefatigably and fearlessly inculcating these principles by speech and writing upon his fellow-countrymen, the influence of his personality upon all Christians speaking the English tongue cannot be estimated too highly. And hence we can discern how it came to pass that the man whom the older Unitarians of America and England regarded with mistrust, and Calvinists and Methodists with abhorrence, while the friends and defenders of slavery at once feared and hated him, no less on account of his classic eloquence, which reminds us of the most admirable models of antiquity, has already, within a few years after his death, come to be revered in every quarter of his vast fatherland as a grand Christian saint and man of God,— nay, also as a prophet of the Christian consciousness regarding the future; and, without doubt, he is destined to exert a still increasing influence, throughout the United States, on the spiritual conception of Christianity and the practical application of its principles.

"Channing is an antique hero with a Christian heart. He is a man like a Hellene, a citizen like a Roman, a Christian like an apostle. People take him for what he is not when they treat him as a learned and speculative theologian."

He then goes on to suggest that in the latter case Channing might have become in some sort a Trinitarian, quotes from the discourses on "The Means of Promoting Christianity," "Sermon on Spiritual Freedom," "Remarks on Life and Character of Napoleon Bonaparte," and "Essay on the Duty of the Free States of North America," and continues: —

"If such a man, whose whole life and conversation, in the sight of all his fellow-citizens, stand in absolute correspondence with the earnestness of his Christian language, and are without a spot, be not a prophet of God's presence in humanity, I know of none such."

I have given Bunsen a section to himself, because he of all men is entitled to speak both in the name of England and of Germany. And now let me speak of Germany alone.

VII. CHANNING'S INFLUENCE IN GERMANY.

(9.) A translation of Channing's Complete Works, by Sydow and Schulze, was published in Berlin in the year 1850, some years before Bunsen published his *God in History;* and it seems to me, after a careful study of Bunsen's later influence in Germany, that, while he may not be willing to accord to Channing the power to give any "scientific solution of the problem of God in history," this great thinker and his friend Richard Rothe approached in later days more nearly to the Christology of Channing than is shown by the book from which I have quoted.

The publication in 1859 of Bunsen's *Signs of the Times* was the starting-point for a new Protestant movement in Germany, the leaders of which were, among lawyers, Dr. Bluntschli, Baron von Holtzendorff, and Hausser; and, among the theologians, Dr. Daniel Schenkel and

Richard Rothe of Heidelberg, and Dr. Carl Schwarz of Gotha, and Baumgarten, Holtzmann, Spaeth, Littel, Krause, Manchot, etc.

While the theological diversities of these men were very great, that *Religion of Conscience*, which as Martineau says sprang to its feet at the bidding of Channing, was the bond of union and the basis of common activity among these men. In 1865, at Eisenach, they constituted the Protestantenverein. Their example was quickly followed by Holland and Hungary; and, at the Conferences of these Associations, delegates from the Church of Channing, both in England and America, have frequently been warmly received and respectfully listened to. While Hase, Gieseler, Pfleiderer, Hagenbach, and many other German writers, have borne their testimony to Channing's influence, we can only let one of them speak here, Nippold, the historian of the Protestantenverein: —

"After Parker, who is widely known by the popular style of his writings,[*] it is especially Channing who claims our attention. The study of Channing's life shows many points of resemblance between him and the great Protestant heroes of Europe. His chief characteristic is the active power of the individual conscience. Like Vinet and Chalmers, he cannot be called an original thinker; but, like them, he insists on the development of individual religion, emphasizing above all things what is seemingly human and common to all individualities rather than the exceptional endowments of genius.

"In all the fundamentals of Channing's theology, the gospel freedom of the Unitarians is as strongly marked as their Christian piety. His anthropology, like that of the Rationalists, is based on the possibility of repentance and improvement, which, however, is not with him, as with them, a matter of philosophic deduction, but the result of his ethical faith in the dignity of man. The Augustinian pessimism of the old orthodoxy is in his eyes a hinderance to the true spirit of Christianity; and he clothes the old rationalistic Trinity, God, Virtue, and Immortality, with a beauty unknown to the Rationalists. Jesus is not for him merely an object of admiration, but also an example that we may follow, whose death has a practical moral value for us, and who has revealed to us the fatherly providence of God.

"While Channing's Christology was essentially Unitarian, and he was brave enough to bear the social odium attached to this name, he was strongly opposed to sectarianism and the prison walls of creeds; seeking the manifestations of Christian character not in them, but in the spirit and life of its professors. He showed his eminently ethical tendencies by his brave antagonism to all social and religious evils, but especially to the spirit of slavery and persecution. With a sincere love for the republican institutions of his birthland, he warns his countrymen against national pride and prejudice; and his horror for the

---

[*] These few words are all that Nippold has to say regarding Parker, while Fock in his *History of Socinianism* has more to say about Parker than about Channing.

excesses of the French Revolution of 1793 is equalled by his benevolent sympathy for the legitimate national aspirations of France, Germany, and Italy. His dislike of party spirit is shown by his repeated warnings against the faults of organizations, while he cordially acknowledges their value within due limits. It was his object not to make men into parts of a machine, but to develop their self-conscious individual energy, not to subject them to external authority, but to win their obedience for the voice of God in conscience. He shows, too, how dangerous the exaggeration of associated action is to the whole community, how far superior are the quiet influences of home life to those of any public institution for children, and how the proper use of natural relations does more to promote Christianity than any official mission. In all these practical questions, he carries out his own fundamental principle, the value of the individual soul; and, just like Vinet, he subordinates to this end all political and ecclesiastical institutions.

"In treating of the elevation of the working classes, he looks, first of all, to their moral, and, secondly, to their material welfare. It is just the same with his care for the prisoners, for the cause of temperance, for seafaring men, and for education. The philanthropist Brownson, Tuckerman, the lover of the lost, Father Taylor, the sailor's evangelist, found in Channing their most ardent sympathizer. No one was more in earnest about keeping holy the Sabbath day than Channing, yet no one was more strongly opposed to the Sabbatarian degradation of Christianity for objects of police than he was.

"Channing has emphasized in America that ethical character of Christianity which has long been insisted on by the noblest minds in Europe. To this the mystical and supernatural aspects of religion are in him subordinate, and its most essential aspect is conscious devotion to what is good. But this devotion must be conscious and self-acting. Channing's virtue is not passive, but active. Patience, humility, self-denial, are inspired by him with robust virility, and suffering is sacred because it is sustained by moral energy. In spite of all Channing's critical, speculative, and æsthetic deficiencies, he is one of the moral heroes of our century, and deserves to be called 'The Unitarian Saint.' And the Unitarians are worthy of their hero. While Gieseler praises them because they have won back to Christianity many a soul alienated from it by the creeds and superstitions of the sects, Wichern has found among the Unitarians some of his most successful and devoted predecessors in the works of practical Christian love. Even Schaff, who regards them as infidels, is obliged to confess that they are as generous as their orthodox neighbors. The great importance of Channing is now recognized in the whole civilized world, after men like Edgar Quinet in France and Bunsen in Germany have drawn attention to it."

(10.) And this influence on Germany has extended far beyond the borders of the Fatherland. Among the Lutheran pastors living far away in Southern Transylvania, among those apostolic laborers who are working under terrible discouragements to keep alive the flame of evangelical Christianity in the little villages of Austrian Galicia and Silesia, in the Baltic provinces of Russia, and among the preachers and professors of Holland, I have found Sydow's translation of Channing; and its possessors have welcomed me when I spoke of him, and have wanted to know more of his people. To Berne, to Basel, and to Zürich, his thought has also gone in German dress.

VIII. France.

Channing's own letters, written in 1831 and 1832 to Baron de Gerando and M. de Sismondi, show his intense interest in the state of religion in France. His own sojourn on the continent helped to make his work known there; and when, after the events of 1848, the grave question of pauperism was agitated among the French publicists, one of them, Laboulaye, was delighted to find, in Channing's paper on the ministry to the poor, the solution so much desired. He published a translation under the title, *Channing, Apostolat auprès des Pauvres*, and soon after, *Channing: Œuvres Sociales. Traduction Laboulaye.* After the appearance of W. H. Channing's memoirs of his uncle, there appeared another work, *Channing: Sa Vie et ses Œuvres, par M. de Rémusat*. And so the words of Channing inspired in France that ministry to the poor, which was carried on in Switzerland by Pestalozzi, in Alsace by Pastor Oberlin, and in Hamburg by Madame Sieveking and Dr. Wichern.

In that martyr Church of France,—dear to us for its sufferings, and for those noble souls, like James Martineau, which it has given to humanity,—there have been many who, like the two Coquerels, Reville, Fontanes, Pressensée, Colani, Vincent, Dide, have not only loved and studied Channing, but have carried the influence of his thought to the French part of Switzerland and to the Walloon Churches of Holland. But Laboulaye and Rémusat are peculiarly important, because their enthusiasm for Channing is free from all theological bias.

Another Frenchman whom we cannot neglect in this connection is M. Renan, whose "Channing et le Mouvement Unitaire aux Etats-Unis," published in his *Etudes d'Histoire Religieuse*, 1863, does as much justice to Channing and to American and English Unitarianism as his non-Christian and specially anti-Protestant bias will permit. To

---

* This publication was reviewed in the principal journals of France and Belgium, especially by Renan in the *Revue des Deux Mondes*, by Leroy in the *Revue de Paris*, and by Pelletan in the *Siècle*; while M. van Niemen in Brussels wrote a study of Channing's Works.

show the spirit of Renan's brilliant essay on Channing, the following quotation will suffice: —

"The special character of France prevents us from supposing that Channing's ideas (except under great restrictions) are applicable to it. They aspire to create an enlightened population rather than a grand culture. But France unites two extremes,— a general vulgarity below mediocrity, and an intellectual aristocracy transcending all others in the world. Channing's religious ideas seem to me just as inappropriate to our country. If France were really capable of creating a national religious movement, she would have become Protestant under the favorable conditions of the seventeenth century. But she has rejected Protestantism. She is the most orthodox country in the world, because she is the most indifferent in religious matters."

Such assertions may impose upon careless observers, who are fascinated by Renan's magnificent style. But are they true?

When a Sylvestre de Sacy bears witness to the historic significance of the French Protestant Church, a Charles de Rémusat to its religious value, an Émile Montegut to its moral influence, an Audiganne and a Baudon to the industrial achievements of the French Protestants, we may be justified in supposing that Renan has not seen the whole truth; and, for my own part, I believe that what may have been wanting to make the Unitarianism of Channing a power in France has been supplied by James Martineau. And now I have to call the attention of our American brethren to a French book upon Channing, which seems to me at once the most affecting, the most interesting, and, in its possible effects for the spread of Channing's influence among the Catholic races of Europe, the most important that has yet appeared. It is entitled *Channing: Sa Vie et sa Doctrine, par René Lavollée. Ouvrage couronné par l'Académie des Sciences Morales et Politiques. Paris*, 1876. Renan's essay was the work of the librarian of Louis Napoleon, too courtly to write what might displease the bigoted empress, and flattering imperial vanity before the bubble had burst.

Lavollée's book is that of a pious Catholic, seeing in Channing the American Fénelon, wishing that the Unitarian saint were a Catholic like himself, writing when the imperial bubble has burst, and earnestly trying to learn from the Americans what he and his fellow-countrymen can do to avert the terrible dangers which threaten modern France. I have sent you to-day my review of this book. So I will now only beg you to tell my American brethren that I see the call of God in it to use the means offered us by Lavollée's essay of bringing Channing's noblest inspirations to bear on our Catholic brethren in Canada, France, Italy, Spain, Portugal, etc., far more persuasively than without Lavollée's aid we could have done it.

Jules Simon's tribute to Channing, mentioned in the preface to this book, is also a most encouraging evidence that the French republicans of to-day are alive to their real duties to their country, and lead us to hope that those misfortunes of 1793 and 1830, which no one deplored more than Channing, will be averted now.

IX. ITALY.

The most characteristic evidence of Channing's influence in Italy is contained in an article by Professor Sbarbaro, published in the *Rivista Europea* of October, 1879. He relates how in 1863 he met at Leghorn a Jewish lady from Manchester (probably Mrs. Schwabe, the friend of John James Tayler), who first drew his attention to Channing's works. He obtained them in Florence, and says:—

"They were to me a revelation, or rather a reminiscence, of ideas which I had long entertained in my own confused and indistinct thought, and which now came before me in orderly elucidation, like the faces of old friends never forgotten.

"No single writer, since Dante, has ever made so great and so profound an impression on my faculties as Channing."

Sbarbaro shows ground for believing that Channing supplies the very form and spirit of that religion which is needed by the craving heart of thoughtful Italy; and he concludes:—

"In fine, I have made choice of Channing as the most eloquent witness, and an irrefragable proof of the new evolution of Christian thought in the world, and of the reform which is being initiated in human religiousness, because, in the story of his career, and in the fortunes of his books, in the marvel of their rapid and universal diffusion in all corners of the civilized earth, is to be seen the most luminous and triumphant proof of the reality of that movement which is inwardly transforming European society, and bringing it little by little to worship under the roof of a new temple, that church really catholic, whose frontal shall bear, without untruth, the inscription, "TO THE ONE GOD," which Mazzini hailed on the façades of the Unitarian Churches of Hungary."

Another sign of the times in Italy is the appearance of Terenzio Mamiani's *La Religione dell' Avvenire: della Religione Positiva e Perpetua del Genere Umano*. Milan, 1880. Mamiani, who became acquainted with Unitarianism through Professor Bracciforti's translation of Channing, advises his countrymen to develop the movement commenced by Bernardino Occhino, of Sienna, and the two Sozzini.

Several other prominent Italians, as Aurelio Saffi, Luigi Luzzati, and Ruggero Bonghi, will speak at the conference to be held in Italy on the birthday of Channing. But, while welcoming these new laborers in the vineyard, we must not forget those older Italian expositors of Channing who have borne the heat and burden of the day: the advocate Magnani, who for years conducted Unitarian service at Pisa; Professor Filopanti, the astronomer, who lectured on Channing's idea of duty, in Bologna, Milan, Rome, and Naples; and Ferdinando Bracciforti, the translator of Channing, who has also for years past conducted a Unitarian church in Florence, and another in Reggio.

X. HUNGARY.

While for about three hundred years there has existed in Transylvania an Episcopalian Unitarian Church, the work of Channing was first communicated to the brethren there by Alexander Farkas, a Unitarian from Klausenburg, who visited Massachusetts in 1831, and afterwards published an account of his American travels. In 1848, the young Transylvanian professor, Joseph Jakab, brother of the learned biographer of Francis Davidis, took home with him, on his return from Manchester New College, the works of Channing, intending to circulate them in Hungary, but was prevented by the war and his early death. In 1852, Sydow's German translation was introduced among the Transylvanian Saxons; and in 1861 the *Kereszteny Magveti* (Christian Seed-sower) contained translations from Channing's works; while the professors of the college, aided by money from Boston, have now translated the complete work into Magyar, and circulated them among Catholics, Calvinists, Lutherans, and Greeks. Professor Moritz Ballagi, the liberal Calvinist, and Peter Hatala, formerly Professor of Theology in the Roman Catholic Seminary of Budapest, now an eloquent advocate of Unitarianism, have both acknowledged their deep obligation to the works of Channing, which are read by men of all churches in Hungary. It will interest you to know that young Count Gerando, grandson of Channing's correspondent of 1832, has in 1875 publicly notified his conversion from the conventional Catholicism of his family and his entry into the Unitarian Church of Hungary.

XI. SCANDINAVIA.

In Sweden there is published a Unitarian religious paper called *Sanningsökaren* (the Truth-seeker), which has a circulation of about two thousand in Sweden, Norway, Denmark, Finland, and Iceland. A recent number, mentioning the enterprise of Mr. Spears, says: "Portions of Channing's works have been translated into Icelandic by M. Jochumson of Reikiavik. A collection of Channing's discourses in a Swedish version was issued as early as 1840, by a congenial spirit, Nils Ignell." I may mention that one of our English Unitarian ministers, Rev. Ephraim Turland of Ainsworth, has made the promotion of Channing's influence in Scandinavia his own special object, and I have asked him to write you direct.

XII. SWITZERLAND.

The German cantons of Switzerland have been always in intimate connection with the German admirers of Channing. Nippold, whose eulogy I have quoted, and Schmidt, a former secretary of the Protestantenverein, are now professors of theology at Swiss universities. The French cantons are in just as intimate connection with the liberal Protestants of Paris; and Etienne Chastel, Professor of Ecclesiastical History at Geneva, and the friend of John James Tayler, is among Channing's most ardent admirers. But French Switzerland has itself produced two great Unitarians,— Samuel Vincent and Alexander Vinet,— who did for French theology what Channing did for New England. Samuel Vincent, after studying Kant, Schleiermacher, and De Wette, put Christianity, like Channing, into relation with the facts of conscience and the wants of the human soul; while Vinet, making Christ the centre of the gospel, also expresses the idea of the New England saint when he says, "The great merit of the Reformation was the restoration to the individual of all his responsibility,— to remove him from the convenient government of the faith of authority, and to impose upon him *the most severe of laws, that of liberty.*"

XIII. HOLLAND.

Holland, like Switzerland and America, always hospitable to those who were exiles for conscience' sake, has never been wanting in the representatives of a free theology since Erasmus John published his *Antitheses Doctrinæ Christi et Antichristi de uno vero Deo.*

Its older liberal school — of which Van der Palm, Heringa, Muntighe, and Clarisse were the chiefs — arrived at the same results as Channing, and by the same methods, while Clarisse resembled him as a man and as preacher.

In the Walloon Churches of Holland, Coquerel, Reville, and Maronnier have made Channing known; and the latter has translated some of his writings into Dutch.

In a work published in London by Dr. E. J. Diest Lorgion, a member of the Gröningen School, Channing is also quoted as an authority in religion.

The foreign missions of the Dutch Missionary Societies are more wisely conducted than any others known to me.

XIV. Russia.

Of the Baltic provinces of Russia, I have already spoken in connection with Germany; of Finland, in connection with Scandinavia.

Though I have heard that some of Channing's works have been translated into Russian, I have no evidence of the fact. So far as the Catholics of Russian Poland are concerned, their great sympathy with France leads me to believe that René Lavollée's book on Channing would find ready acceptance among them, while I can form no opinion as to the people who are under the tyranny of the Russo-Greek priesthood.

XV. Spain and Portugal and their Colonies.

Here I have not discovered any traces of Channing's influence, and in regard to them I would refer to what I have already said about Lavollée's book.

XVI. Greece, Turkey, Syria, Egypt.

In these countries, the American missions might be used as a means of propagandism. And I think it especially desirable that a selection from Channing should be translated into the language of the Koran.

XVII. In Conclusion.

I have tried in the foregoing report to confine myself as much as possible to the published evidence of other men, carefully keeping my own subjective convictions in the background.

I cannot, however, conclude without expressing my own conviction that we have in the works of Channing an aid to missionary effort, in the circulation of which all schools of Unitarians can unite, and which is likely to be welcomed by people of every church and country. Let us, however, in using it, carefully examine all that has been written about Channing in every country in which his books have been read, and, as far as possible, adapt our selections from Channing to the necessities of time and place.

You in Brooklyn are at the gate of America, and have the best opportunity of influencing those who come from the Old World as immigrants, and who come to the Old World as visitors. And I would earnestly suggest to you the propriety of having selections from Channing in the chief European languages, or the best essays on Channing existing in these languages,—as Sbarbaro's in Italian, Sydow's or Manchot's in German, Lavollée's in French,—distributed, at the lowest possible price, wherever they can do any good.

Yours very cordially.

JOHN FRETWELL.

Cordial letters, expressive of interest in the celebration and of regret at not being able to attend its meetings, were received from numerous other friends: Charles W. Eliot, LL.D., President of Harvard University; ex-Governor George S. Boutwell, of Massachusetts; Henry P. Kidder, Esq., President of the American Unitarian Association; John. H. Rogers, Esq., of Boston; Col. Thomas Wentworth Higginson; Dr. W. F. Channing; Miss Mary Channing; Prof. J. L. Diman, of Brown University; Rev. E. A. Washburn, D.D., New York; Rev. W. H. Furness, D.D.; Rev. R. P. Stebbins, D.D.; Rev. James Freeman Clarke, D.D.; Rev. L. D. Bevan, D.D., of New York; Rev. E. E. Hale, D.D.; Rev. Messrs. J. F. W. Ware, R. R. Shippen, Samuel Longfellow, S. R. Calthrop, Minot J. Savage, Brooke Herford, James De Normandie, C. A. Staples, C. G. Ames, H. H. Barber, E. H. Hall, etc.

RESOLUTIONS.

At a meeting of the Second Unitarian Church, Brooklyn, held in their chapel on April 11, the following preamble and resolutions were unanimously adopted:—

Whereas, The Centennial Celebration of Channing's Birthday, as devised and carried out by the First Unitarian Society in this city, has proved an occasion in the highest degree satisfactory to all concerned, therefore,—

Resolved, That we, the members of the Second Unitarian Society, heartily congratulate Dr. Putnam and the people of his church on the success of their enterprise, and on the honor they have done themselves in honoring the great memory of Channing; and that we are sincerely obliged to them, not only for their generous hospitality to us, but for the occasion generally, promotive, as it has proved, of so much earnest thought and kindly feeling.

Resolved, That copies of these Resolutions be transmitted to Dr. Putnam and to the Clerk of his Society.

At a meeting of the First Unitarian Church, Brooklyn, held after the regular morning service, on Sunday, April 18, 1880, the following preamble and resolutions, presented by the pastor, were unanimously adopted:—

Whereas, The Pastor and Secretary of this Society have received copies of the Resolutions which the Second Church unanimously adopted last Sunday morning, congratulating the First Church on the success of the recent Channing Celebration in this city, and thanking its members "for their generous hospitality," and "for the occasion generally, promotive, as it has proved, of so much earnest thought and kindly feeling," —

Resolved, That we warmly reciprocate the friendly sentiments thus conveyed to us from the Second Church, and heartily return our grateful acknowledgments to its minister, Rev. Mr. Chadwick, for the fine Centennial Ode which he read at the Memorial Meeting; and to him and his parishioners both, for the active interest and cordial sympathy with which they greatly encouraged and aided the enterprise we had in hand.

Resolved. That the Secretary of this Church be instructed to send to Mr. Chadwick and the Clerk of his Society copies of these Resolutions.

NOTICES OF THE PRESS.

THE following editorials, taken from the leading daily papers of Brooklyn of April 8, indicate the interest which the meetings of the celebration awakened in the public mind, and the general sympathy with which the occasion was regarded by the people of the city:—

THE CHANNING CENTENARY.

The Channing centenary celebration in Brooklyn came to a conclusion last evening at the Academy of Music, and proved to be a far warmer and more remarkable occasion than some of the scientific observers of thought had anticipated. Indeed, to those who maintained that Unitarianism had lost its lustre upon the minds of men, and was fast fading out of the denominational galaxy, that its cold intellectuality was fatal to its existence, the celebration in this city must have been a surprise. Clergymen of all denominations gathered upon the platform last evening to do honor to the courageous and noble-minded man whose name stands for the creed which, even in our own day, boasts so many men of character and intellect; and this fact alone would seem to silence those who looked pityingly and half-contemptuously upon Unitarianism as an experiment tried, and found to be unsatisfactory. Mr. Beecher, for one, made one of the best addresses of his life in pointing out the changes that had come over the world in respect of sectarian religion, by referring to the attitude toward one another of Channing and the Rev. Lyman Beecher. Considerably less than a century ago, these two warriors of the church were exchanging blows, because they could not look at life precisely in the same way, or because the same methods of spiritual development did not suit both equally well. At this time, representatives of all denominations met to celebrate Channing's birth; and the son of his old theological antagonist was the most ardent of all. As Mr. Beecher declared, the religion of to-day is vastly changed from what it was. It is no longer a machine. The machinery of ritual, of pomp, of dogma, had done its work in fostering the religious sentiment by impressing the sense of duty, of veneration, and of morality; but, having done that, its work was ended. Thoughtful men have at length discovered that religion is not a system to be defined: it is, in fact, philologically incapable of definition. But, having made that discovery, the thinking men of to-day have been led to look, not upon the machinery, but the result of its operations: not upon the creed, but upon the man. As Mr. Beecher put it, "The church was made for man, not man for the church"; and, when one man appears whose religious sense was as conspicuously and perfectly developed as was the imaginative faculty in Shakspeare or Milton, all religious men meet to celebrate his birth without inquiring what religious university he graduated from, or protesting that he would have been a better or a greater man, had he been a Catholic, a Presbyterian, a Buddhist, or a Jew. In other words, conformity to the Christian ideal is better tested by works of beneficence, by purity of life, and the love of one's fellow-men, than by a vast and comprehensive knowledge of dialectics, and an ability to spell the Westminster catechism backward. When one sees the leaders of all creeds, and hears the thoughts of these men expressed as they were last night, one may acquiesce, for a time at least, in the belief that the brotherhood of mankind is not a vague ideality, but a fact already accomplished and almost generally discerned. We commend the report of last evening's exercises to all our readers. — *Brooklyn Eagle.*

THE CHANNING MEMORIAL.

The interest of the people of Brooklyn in the services commemorative of William Ellery Channing was indeed surprising. This is not a monument-rearing age, and the tombs of the prophets go unrepaired and unhonored. But the name of Channing acted as a spell to break the ice of forgetfulness and to cast down the barriers of creed. It was felt that he represented a new era of religious thought, in which there were a larger freedom and a broader toleration. Even half a century ago, such meetings as these, that for two days interested Brooklyn, would have been impossible. Such sentiments of brotherhood and unity could not have been uttered and found a cordial response. Indeed, even now, as was freely admitted, were Channing alive, such a demonstration would be impossible. Were Channing a Brooklyn pastor to-day, the children of his Sunday-school could have no part in the annual gatherings in which the Sunday-schools of the evangelical pastors who took part in yesterday's services freely participate. This wall of partition may possibly disappear within the next century. But, while it stands, it is to be hoped that no *enfant terrible* will astonish his Sunday-school teacher by promulgating a conundrum suggested by these obvious inconsistencies. The influences of such a day as yesterday ought to be of permanent good. It is not easy, but it is not impossible, to carry into the conduct of ecclesiastical affairs somewhat of the spirit that animated these meetings, and which met with such a hearty response from an audience in which every social, political, and ecclesiastical interest in Brooklyn found a place. The gathering last night was immense in size and in enthusiasm, and was every way representative of all the phases of Brooklyn life. It was a marked exhibition of the various strata of our social organization, as distinct and clear as a rift that should sever the earth's crust and leave the successive formations exposed from the latest to the earliest geological periods. It was not mere curiosity that drew these people there, and kept them together for more than three hours. There was a profound sympathy in the occasion, and with all that was said, that was timely and appropriate; and there was a yearning for just such a condition of accord as that which Channing's life prefigured, and for that freedom which, in his words, "casts off all fear but that of wrong-doing."—*Brooklyn Union-Argus.*

We may also add the following brief extracts from several of the religious weeklies:—

Of all the demonstrations in honor of Channing, none have been more imposing and impressive than the celebration in the city of Brooklyn, the arrangements of which were chiefly in the hands of Rev. Dr. A. P. Putnam, minister of the Church of the Saviour. The observances consisted of meetings in the church on Tuesday evening and Wednesday morning, and a monster meeting in the Academy of Music on

Wednesday evening. The fit and happy key was struck in inviting and securing the co-operation of all classes, without distinction of sect, though the Unitarians naturally took a leading part.

Christian Register (Unitarian), Boston.

The Channing celebration in Brooklyn, which extended over two days, developed at its close one of the most remarkable public meetings ever held in this country. There sat on the platform of the Academy of Music leading and accepted representative men of the Episcopal, the Methodist, Baptist, Congregational, and Presbyterian churches, in full and hearty sympathy with the whole movement. It was not a meeting organized by all or any one of these denominations, to which select and pious clergymen of Unitarian affinities had been invited. It was a Unitarian platform, conducted by a Unitarian gentleman, for a celebration in honor of the great high priest of Unitarianism in America; and, though there was on the part of the Unitarian [Trinitarian?] speakers a distinct recognition of Channing as a theologian who was not of their school, it was not said in any apologetic way. The audience crowded the large house from the platform or stage to the very ceiling, occupying the seats and every inch of standing room, and remained intact from eight o'clock until nearly half-past eleven.

Christian Union (Orthodox Congregational), New York.

The following is an extract from a letter of Rev. Almon Gunnison, the New York correspondent of the *Christian Leader* (Universalist), Boston:—

The most notable event that has taken place for many years in this vicinity was the recent Channing Memorial. The exercises commenced on Tuesday night, with a calm, able, discriminating sermon from Dr. Peabody. On Wednesday morning, Dr. Putnam's church was filled with the members and clergy of all denominations. So many were there who had a word to say, that it was not possible to bring the meeting to a close until two o'clock, when, notwithstanding the fact that many went to their homes, over six hundred were entertained at lunch in the chapel. This noonday collation was a thing to be remembered for its hospitality and elegance. The room was a bower of beauty, rich with floral decorations and delicacy of arrangement and service. The festival culminated in the grand gathering of the evening. The vast Academy of Music was literally crowded to suffocation, four thousand being present. Never before have we seen in that famous place of meeting such a gathering. Judges, mayors, leading citizens of every creed, the wealth and refinement of the two cities, were there; while upon the stage were the leading clergymen of all the denominations. We carefully noted the fact that, strange as the concord of the meeting seemed, it was not thought strange. The unwonted unity was hardly alluded to; it was taken as a matter of course. The echoes of that grand meeting yet make their sweet music in our hearts; and the vision of that vast assembly, sitting together in the unity of spirit, seems like the foregleams of the millennial day, when men of every name and nation shall sit down together in the kingdom of heaven.

www.ingramcontent.com/pod-product-compliance
Lightning Source LLC
Chambersburg PA
CBHW020908230426
43666CB00008B/1355